ESTRENO Collection of Contemporary Spanish Plays

General Editor: Phyllis Zatlin

AUTUMN FLOWER

(Flor de Otoño)

"Flor de Otoño," Barcelona performer. 1932.
As reprinted in *Primer Acto*, October 1974.

JOSÉ MARÍA RODRÍGUEZ MÉNDEZ

AUTUMN FLOWER

(*Flor de Otoño*)

Translated by Marion Peter Holt

ESTRENO Plays
New Brunswick, New Jersey
2001

ESTRENO Contemporary Spanish Plays 20
General Editor: Phyllis Zatlin
                 Department of Spanish & Portuguese
                 Faculty of Arts & Sciences
                 Rutgers, The State University of New Jersey
                 105 George Street
                 New Brunswick, New Jersey 08901-1414 USA

Library of Congress Cataloging in Publication Data
Rodríguez Méndez, José María
   Autumn Flower
   Bibliography:
   Contents: Autumn Flower.
Translation of: Flor de Otoño.
   1. Rodríguez Méndez, José María, 1925   Translation, English.
I. Holt, Marion Peter. II. Title.
Library of Congress Catalog Card No.: 00-130967
ISBN: 1-888463-12-0

© 2001 Copyright by ESTRENO
Original play © José María Rodríguez Méndez: Flor de Otoño, 1974, 1979, 1983.
Translation © Marion Peter Holt, 2001

First edition

All rights reserved
No part of this publication may be reproduced or transmitted in any form or by any means, electronic or mechanical, including photocopy, recording, or any information storage or retrieval system now known or to be invented, without permission in writing from the publishers, except by a reviewer who wishes to quote brief passages in connection with a review written for inclusion in a magazine, newspaper, or broadcast.

> The publishers wish to acknowledge with thanks
> financial assistance for this translation from the
> Dirección General del Libro, Archivos y Bibliotecas
> del Ministerio de Educación y Cultura de España.

Cover: Jeffrey Eads

A NOTE ON THE PLAY

In *Autumn Flower*, playwright José María Rodríguez Méndez's juxtaposes two (presumably) mutually exclusive milieus: the world of a wealthy aristocratic Catalonian family and the Barcelona underworld, circa 1930. The family is lead by a strong-minded matriarch, Doña Nuria de Canellas, the widow of a wealthy industrialist, who insists on maintaining the appearance of family honor and respectability at all cost. On the other hand, the Barcelona underworld is inhabited by gangsters, anarchists, low-lifes, and other so-called disreputable people who frequent the clubs of the Barrio Chino.

The two worlds of the play converge in the iconoclastic central figure, Flor de Otoño, or Autumn Flower, a cabaret performer who never seems far from trouble. Early in the play, for example, he is implicated in the murder of a rival performer, yet seems to elude scandal—or prosecution. It soon becomes clear that he leads a double life. Flor de Otoño is the stage persona of Lluiset, a respected lawyer and the son of Doña Nuria de Canellas. Lluiset and his alter ego have a mutually exploitative relationship: he inhabits and manipulates one milieu by exploiting the other.

His objective, however, is not to protect his identity in each milieu as one might think; rather, he plays one against the other to obscure a darker truth. His double life—bourgeois lawyer and female impersonator—camouflages his activities as an anarchist. But whether he is committed to violent political change remains uncertain at play's end; Flor de Otoño appears to incite more riots than fight them.

To complicate this picture, the author sets the play during a time of heightened tension between Catalonians and Castilians. It is based on figures from actual news stories—but only loosely. Rodríguez Méndez is more interested in myth-making than documentation, and imbues his story with a sense of mystery and ambiguity. There is an indelible atmosphere to the play, due, in part, to social environment, class distinctions, and quirky character roles written in both Castilian and Catalan. In part it is due to the locale; Barcelona is as much a character in the play as Lluiset. The author has created a feeling for the various elements that made the city such a hotbed of political activity prior to the civil war.

Still, at the center of this picture is an unusual character in Spanish drama: a gay protagonist who confidently exploits his culture's assumptions about gender to subvert the culture from the inside.

Michael Kinghorn
Dramaturg
Alliance Theatre Company

JOSÉ MARÍA RODRÍGUEZ MÉNDEZ

ABOUT THE PLAYWRIGHT

José María Rodríguez Méndez (b. 1925) is best known for his plays that present moments of Spain's social history as seen "from below," from the perspective of the marginalized and oppressed who are its victims. These victims include young soldiers in *Vagones de madera* (*Wooden Train Cars*, 1959), carted off to serve as cannon fodder in Spain's colonial wars in North Africa, Andalusian peasants in *La batalla de Verdún* (*The Battle of Verdun*, 1965), forced to emigrate to work in Barcelona's factories, as well as the degraded masses pictured in *Bodas que fueron famosas del Pingajo y la Fandanga* (*The Famous Nuptials of Pingajo and Fandanga*, 1968). Long censorsed for its ridicule of the army—an untouchable institution in Franco's Spain—this last play was selected to inaugurate Madrid's new National Theatre Center in 1978.

Rodríguez Méndez's plays are often chronicles that incorporate elements of Spain's popular culture and language. *Historia de unos cuantos* (*Story of a Few People*, 1976), depicts ten moments in Spain's history as seen through the eyes of characters taken from *zarzuelas* or popular light operas. *The Famous Nuptials*, set in a Madrid shanty town of 1898, chronicles the "exploits" of a scarecrow soldier in rags, just back from the war in Cuba, and his innocent child bride, incorporating popular sketches that recreate the atmosphere of the *zarzuela* and *sainete* or brief farce. However, the bitter epilogue recalls Valle-Inclán's *esperpentos* or grotesque caricatures as Pingajo is executed and buried, wrapped in a tattered Spanish flag. *Autumn Flower* (1982), set in Barcelona's redlight district of the 1930s, was inspired by a real transvestite singer and anarchist gunman, known as "Flor de Otoño," about whom Rodríguez Méndez had read in newspaper accounts of the time. These chronicles, with their succession of popular sketches and narrative structure, represented a new dramatic model in post-Civil War Spain that owed much to Brecht.

Rodríguez Méndez has also authored dramatic homages to figures from Spain's Golden Age of arts and letters: Cervantes, Teresa de Avila, and Juan de la Cruz. In 1994 he won the National Theatre Prize for *El pájaro solitario* (*The Solitary Bird*) which portrays a half-delirious John of the Cross who escapes his jailers and is befriended by whores and rufians who are strangely touched by his poetry.

Martha T. Halsey
Penn State University

CAUTION: Professionals and amateurs are hereby warned that *Autumn Flower* is subject to a royalty. The play is fully protected under the copyright laws of the United States of America, and of all countries covered by the International Copyright Union (including the Dominion of Canada and the rest of the British Commonwealth), and of all countries covered by the Pan-American Copyright Convention and the Universal Copyright Convention, and of all countries with which the United States has reciprocal copyright relations. All rights, including professional and amateur staging, motion picture, recitation, public reading, radio broadcasting, television, video or sound taping, and all other forms of mechanical or electronic reproduction, such as information storage and retrieval systems and photocopying, and the rights of translation into foreign languages, are strictly reserved

All inquiries regarding performances of *Autumn Flower* in English and other permissions should be addressed to the translator's agent:

Barbara Hogenson Agency
165 West End Avenue. Suite 19-C
New York, NY 10023
(212) 874-8084; Fax (212) 362-3011
E-Mail: BHogenson@aol.com

General inquiries may be addressed to the translator: Marion Peter Holt, 133 West 71st. Street, Apt. 7-B, New York NY 10023. E-Mail: mpholt7@aol.com.

Inquiries to the author regarding *Flor de Otoño* should be made through his representative:

Director de Artes Escénicas y Musicales
Sociedad de Autores y Editores
Calle Fernando VI, No. 4
28004 Madrid, Spain.
Fax: 011-34-91-349 97 12.

Flor de Otoño received its world premiere at the Teatro Principal of Valencia before opening at the Teatro Español of Madrid on 14 December 1982, under the direction of Antonio Díaz Zamora. Sets, costumes and lighting designed by Carlos Cytrinowsky.

Flor de Otoño received its French premiere on 25 January 1992 at the University of Toulouse-Le Mirail, in a staging by Les Anachroniques.

Written in 1972, the play was made into the 1977 movie *Un hombre llamado "Flor de Otoño*," dir. Pedro Olea.

CHARACTERS

At the Serracant Family Home:

DOÑA NURIA DE CAÑELLAS
LLUISET, her son
PILAR, the servant
A FAT, BALD GENTLEMAN, Lluiset's uncle
A SKINNY GENTLEMAN, Lluiset's uncle
A BLOND LADY, Lluiset's aunt
A PLUMP LADY, Lluiset's aunt
A HUNCHBACKED GENTLEMAN, Lluiset's uncle

At the Municipal Office:

SECRETARY
USHER

At the Bataclán Cabaret:

FLOR DE OTOÑO (Lluiset)
RICARD
SURROCA
THE DOORMAN
THE CLOAKROOM ATTENDANT
A WAITER
THE WIDOWER OF "LA ASTURIANITA"
POLICEMEN
PUBLIC (in general)

At the Atarazanas Barracks:

A LIEUTENANT
A CORPORAL
A MEDIC
SEVERAL STREET THUGS
TWO PROSTITUTES

At the Poble Nou Workers' Cooperative:

THE BAR GIRL
A CATALAN PORTER
AN ANDALUSIAN PORTER
A GALICIAN PORTER
A MURCIAN PORTER
FIRST STUDENT
SECOND STUDENT
THIRD STUDENT
FIRST CIVIL GUARD
SECOND CIVIL GUARD
WORKERS

At the Montjuïc Military Prison:

A PRIEST WHO SERVES AS BROTHER OF PEACE AND CHARITY
THE LIEUTENANT-DEFENDER
THE COMMANDER OF THE FORTRESS
A SENTINEL

Street People:

A NIGHT WATCHMAN
TWO MEMBERS OF THE SECRET POLICE
A MODISTE AND HER GUY
A CHORUS GIRL FROM THE SUGRANYES THEATRE COMPANY
LADIES AND GENTLEMEN OF HIGH SOCIETY, etc.

ACTION: In Barcelona, during the early months of 1930

Flor de Otoño, Teatro Español, Madrid, December 1982. Dir. Antonio Díaz Zamora. Set design by Carlos Cytrinowsky. Photo by Manuel Martínez Muñoz.

PART ONE

*Our story begins in the month of January in the year of Our Lord 1930, in a bourgeois residence in the newer fashionable area of Barcelona known as the "Eixample." A cold moonlit night. It, the moon, is reflected, bluish and mysterious, in the mirrors of the parlor of **SEÑORA CAÑELLAS**, widow of a member of the Maurist government, Don Lluís de Serracant, son, in turn, of a general. Consequently, the widow Serracant would have it good, due not only to the pension of the deceased, but to that sense of foresight for which the Catalans have always been famous. The parlor of **SEÑORA NURIA CAÑELLAS**, lit by the moon's reflections, in the wee hours of a cold January night, tells the "what," the "how" and the "why" of the life of its inhabitants. Affluent middle class, proclaimed by that fireplace of white marble in which the embers of the last fire still glow; on the mantelpiece an array of chiming clocks, Chinese porcelain, and some mementos of the Phillipine campaigns of her late husband's companions. The general himself presides on the wall above, in a lunar halo and a bit of urban reflection, since we are, of course, in a second floor apartment. A beautiful Persian rug. Chairs and sofa of garnet-colored plush. Gilded objects. Cornucopias. A framed document with the fawning inscriptions of subordinates. Faded photographs of ladies as they leave the Liceu Opera House. Butterflies fastenened to the wall (sign of the cult of nature characteristic of the nation). A piano. A bronze page boy, a complex mixture of Cupid and Mercury, raises a filigreed torch. The street life penetrates the thick panes of the "tribuna" (that is what they call bay windows in Barcelona), glass of bright oriental colors, a whiff of the Bosphorus, set in filigreed stone in the style of Gaudí. The moonlight, as it enters through the stained glass, forms beautiful rainbows, which define for us the formality and solidity of a house that stands firm in this year of 1930—although it is obliged to change color according to the eternal and unavoidable phases of the moon.*

August silence. At such an hour, in this house, people are respectably asleep in their beds The only sound is a streetcar. The furtive passing of an automobile. The clatter of a coach that is bringing ladies and gentlemen from the Liceu. Some drunks singing a ditty that goes like this: "Muggers and bums all want their way, so watch your ass or be on your way, muggers and bums. . . ." Tunes of Catalanized Murcians or vice versa, who are so plentiful in these times in which God knows where we'll end up. The photograph of His Majesty King Alfonso XIII, signed with his elegant rubric, seems to shudder before these excesses, but the nearby presence of a Child Jesus under a bell glass, amid paper flowers fashioned by the dear ministering nuns, helps the monarch keep his composure.

And in this harmonious silence, suddenly, unexpectedly, the sound of a doorbell shakes the whole house. A plebeian, coarse, vulgar, unforgiving, criminally loud ring that makes everything reel. The king's picture trembles, the mustache of the elegant general painted in oils trembles, the Child Jesus trembles, the paper flowers. One loud ring and another loud ring. How is it possible that anyone would dare to call in this way at a decent house at such an hour? Unheard of. The action proves to be so unheard of that nothing, nor anyone, responds to such a call. Is no one at home? So it seems. But no. At the tenth ringing of the bell, we now hear voices, sounds, anxiety. We can hear a distraught, indignant woman's exclamation: "Really! . . . But what is this?" Something is approaching this realm of broken silence. The ringing bell has set in motion a whole mechanism of gasping, footsteps, and coughs.

DISTRAUGHT WOMAN'S VOICE: But, Pilar! What are you doing? Ai, deu! Dear Jesus! . . .
ANOTHER WOMAN'S VOICE: I'm coming, ma'am, I'm coming! Oh, dear God! . . .
FIRST VOICE: Go to the door, see who it is! Pilar!
SECOND VOICE: I'm going, ma'am!
FIRST VOICE: See who it is!

(The bell rings and rings. Now there is a tense, terrible, expectant pause. And immediately the servant's melodramatic scream.)

SECOND VOICE: Ay, robbers! They're breaking in!
FIRST VOICE: Ai, mare meva! . . . *(Sounds of footsteps advancing toward the parlor.)*
A MAN'S VOICE *(Which muffles the voices of the women)*: Be quiet, lady, just be quiet for a minute! *(In another tone)* You stay here . . . Hey, you!
FIRST VOICE: Really!
ANOTHER MAN'S VOICE: Which way, Don Ambrosio?
FIRST MAN'S VOICE: I said be quiet, lady! What's wrong with you? Are you crazy?

*(It is at this moment that **DOÑA NURIA CAÑELLAS** bursts in amid the frou-frou and commotion of a most elegant negligee, in slippers and hair dishevelled. **SHE** moves like a wind storm toward the bay window, so blind that **SHE** doesn't realize that in her haste the edge of her sleeve has gotten*

caught on the picture of Don Alfonso XIII, which rolls across the floo
opens a window and, without a second thought, screams:)

DOÑA NURIA: Vigilant! Watchman! . . .Watchman! . . . Help! Thieve.
Thieves!

*(And directly behind her, the **WATCHMAN**, whom **DOÑA NURIA** is invoking, enters the parlor with his navy blue uniform and green braid. Behind the **WATCHMAN** move other forms who look like Chicago gangsters.)*

WATCHMAN: Estic ací, senyora . . . Senyora, can't you see I'm here? *(**HE** grabs her arm and **SHE** turns around and looks at him in amazement.)* I'm here, lady.
DOÑA NURIA: But, really!
WATCHMAN: It's obvious . . . I've come up with the gentlemen. *(And **HE** points to the two figures who are in the doorway leaning against the glass door, breathing hard over their lush moustaches, fed up from ringing the bell and, after so much hassle, eager to finish the night in the Barrio Chino.)* These gents are from . . .
DOÑA NURIA *(Cutting him off)*: They're gangsters!

(One of the moustached men has had enough and steps forward arrogantly toward Doña Nuria.)

FIRST POLICEMAN: From the secret police, señora. *(And the big rogue bows to her.)*
DOÑA NURIA: You don't say! You're obviously gangsters!
WATCHMAN: Now, listen, senyora . . . Ascolti!

*(The **FIRST POLICEMAN**, winking to the other man, has begun to search the entire room with newfound enthusiasm. The first thing **HE** has done is pick up the broken picture of Alfonso XIII, and **HE** looks at it. The **OTHER MAN** lifts up chairs, opens drawers, etc. **DOÑA NURIA** is stupefied.)*

DOÑA NURIA: Well? . . . Is this what the revolution's like? Mare meva santísima! . . . *(**SHE** faints into the arms of the **WATCHMAN**, who has tried unsuccessfully to show her the search warrant.)*
WATCHMAN: Up, up! . . . We're right here . . .
FIRST POLICEMAN *(While **HE** continues his search)*: Give her a few pats on the back.

..D POLICEMAN (*To the FIRST*): Look, a pistol . . . (*Shows it to him.*)
.' POLICEMAN: Let's see.
.TCHMAN (*Who has put DOÑA NURIA on the sofa*): Senyora, listen! . . . The other lady? . . . And the maid?

(*Behind the French doors, the form of a weeping creature is already peering through, not daring to move a step; but seeing DOÑA NURIA'S body lying on the sofa, SHE crosses the frontier of the parlor in a flash of bravery.*)

PILAR: Señora! . . . Señora! Oh, they've killed my lady!
SECOND POLICEMAN: What the hell! Another one.
WATCHMAN: It's nothing, girl . . . It's nothing at all. She's just fainted!
PILAR: Heaven help us! . . .
WATCHMAN: Rub her shoulders, girl . . .

(*Now we have the whole scene set: the SEÑORA in her faint, the SERVANT in distress, the WATCHMAN handling a tough situation, and the POLICEMEN doing their thing. And the entire scene becomes still, creating a chiaroscuro illustration from a novel. Until suddenly the LADY OF THE HOUSE gives a start and sits up abruptly. Her opulent figure stands out in the shadows like a violated queen, her night robe falling off her shoulder. Now the scene is lit by the chandelier and the torch of the "Boy-Mercury" that PILAR and the COPS have been turning on.*)

DOÑA NURIA (*Advancing majestically toward the POLICEMEN*): My dear sirs . . .
WATCHMAN: Listen, this business is . . . well . . .
PILAR: Try to be calm, ma'am . . .
DOÑA NURIA (*To the WATCHMAN and PILAR*): Out of my way! (*And her arm as SHE warns them to step back recalls a gesture by that great actress María Guerrero. To the POLICEMEN who are going about their business turning the room upside down.*). My dear sirs!
FIRST POLICEMAN (*Turning around to her*): We're ready. One second more, lady.
DOÑA NURIA (*Now really angry*): Really, now!
WATCHMAN (*To the POLICEMAN*): Tell her you're only following orders, man . . .
SECOND POLICEMAN: That's a waste of time, friend.
DOÑA NURIA: I'm in my own home! . . . This is my house! I am the widow Serracant!
PILAR (*Like an echo*): This is the house of the widow Serracant!

DOÑA NURIA: In spite of the fact the dictatorship has ended, thank God, I believe you are invading my home.
FIRST POLICEMAN (*Wiping his hands and carrying the broken photograph of Alfonso XIII under his arm*): Yep, señora, that's right. Exactly what you said. (*Indicating the WATCHMAN*): Here's the search warrant. A search warrant for the house of Señor Luis de Serracant y Cañellas and ... (*Taking another paper from his pocket*) this summons requiring said individual to appear in person at the district police station.
SECOND POLICEMAN: Hurry up! We're finished here!

(*The words spoken rapidly and on the run, but with clarity, have left the illustrious lady utterly speechless.*)

WATCHMAN (*Who takes the paper with the summons that DOÑA NURIA has ignored and reads*): "I hereby inform you that you are to appear ... "
DOÑA NURIA (*Angrily and knocking the paper from the WATCHMAN'S hand*): Prou! Enough, I said, enough! Do you hear me? Enough, enough, and enough! ...

(*The POLICEMEN have already done their work and ransacked the place. THEY are carrying off several things: the royal picture, a pistol, some papers.*)

FIRST POLICEMAN (*Bowing to DOÑA NURIA*): Your servant, señora.
DOÑA NURIA: Gangsters, foreigners, traitors!
WATCHMAN: Senyora, senyora! ...
SECOND POLICEMAN: Look at the old gal!
FIRST POLICEMAN: I'm one who's seen it all in my job, had my "ass scraped" as you Catalans say—if you'll pardon the expression. So I don't feel offended and won't run you in for disrespecting an officer. So why don't you just go for a little walk over at the International Exposition.
DOÑA NURIA: You uncouth swine! ...
PILAR (*In an act of extraordinary daring, SHE goes toward the POLICEMAN and strikes him on his lapels with her fists*): Don't insult my lady, nobody insults my lady! ...
DOÑA NURIA (*Holding the weeping servant to her bosom.*): Don't cry, child, don't cry ... (*And her voice breaks.*)
FIRST POLICEMAN: You must respect, señora, that ...
WATCHMAN: They're only doing their job, senyora ...
DOÑA NURIA: Get out, thieves ... thugs, predators!

FIRST POLICEMAN: We've done what we came for. (*To his* ***COMPANION***) Time to go, pal. (*To* ***DOÑA NURIA***) And see if you can take better care of your little boy and keep him out of the Barrio Chino.

(*This said,* ***HE*** *exits. The words "Barrio Chino" in relation to "your little boy" linger in* ***DOÑA NURIA'S*** *mind. A door slams announcing the departure of the* ***POLICEMEN***. *The* ***WATCHMAN*** *doesn't know what to do.*)

DOÑA NURIA (*Asking the* ***SERVANT***): What did they say about the Barrio Chino?
PILAR: Oh, I'm sick, I'm getting siiick! . . .
WATCHMAN; Senyora, what they said, don't pay it any mind.
DOÑA NURIA: What are you doing here? Who called you? Huh?
WATCHMAN: Ascolti, senyora, jo . . .
DOÑA NURIA: What are you doing here? Leave this house! Some watchman you are, some watchman! (*The* ***WATCHMAN*** *steps back in fright.*) A watchman-thug, that's what you are. Just wait, Christmas will come again. And one of these days, you'll be expecting a tip. And we'll give you a tip, just wait.

(*The* ***WATCHMAN*** *has retreated and exited like a soul led off by the devil. Now the two women, in the throes of early morn, look at each other, utter a cry and fall into each other's arms weeping. After a moment,* ***DOÑA NURIA*** *pulls away with a certain revulsion and screams.*)

DOÑA NURIA: The jewels! The jewels! My jewels! (*There is a noisy clatter as* ***SHE*** *opens chests and desk drawers in her search.*) They're here, yes, they haven't taken them . . . my pendant, my rings.
PILAR (*Tearful*): They've taken His Majesty's picture! . . .
DOÑA NURIA: The pendant from Montecarlo, my mother's earrings. (***SHE*** *turns around suddenly and cries out.*) And my boy? Where is my boy?
PILAR: At the Liceu, ma'am. It's his opera night . . .

(***DOÑA NURIA*** *runs to the telephone and dials a number.* ***SHE*** *is nervous.* ***SHE*** *dials again.*)

PILAR: I'm going to heat some water for herb tea.
DOÑA NURIA: You drink it. You need it more than I do . . . (*On the phone*) Montse, is that you Montse? Isn't Montse there? (*Aside*) Oh my, mare de Deu Santísima!
PILAR: Just a little sip of camomile . . .

DOÑA NURIA (*Pushing her away*): Leave me alone! (*To the telephone*) Oh, Montse. Ascolta, nena. Have you seen Lluiset? . . . Yes, yes . . . So was he at the opera? . . . Yes . . . I don't want to hear about Toti dal Monte! At supper afterwards? It's just . . . yes, yes . . . But listen to me. (*Putting her hand over the phone but calmer*) Oh, Montse tries my patience.
PILAR (*Approaching with a tray and tea service*): The camomile . . .
DOÑA NURIA: Montse, will you just listen to me, dona, do you know what happened to me? . . . Something happened . . . (*The lights dim.*)

After total blackout, a page from a newspaper is projected. In bold headlines: "HORRIBLE CRIME IN THE BARRIO CHINO. THE FEMALE IMPERSONATOR KNOWN AS 'LA ASTURIANITA' IS FOUND DEAD IN A PRIVATE ROOM OF THE CRIOLLA CAFE." *In smaller letters:* "*In the early hours of Saturday, the body of Arsenio Puig Bellacasa, known in the underworld by the alias 'La Asturianita,' was found horribly mutilated in a dive known as La Criolla. The Crime was apparently the result of amorous rivalry, although the possibility of anarchist or Free Union involvement is not ruled out. The police are investigating to apprehend the murderer.*" *In smaller headlines:* "*IT IS RUMORED THAT A PRESTIGIOUS INDIVIDUAL FROM OUR BEST SOCIETY HAD A CONNECTION WITH THE MURDER OF 'LA ASTURIANITA.'*" "*Unconfirmed reports indicate that the authorities have a lead in the horrible crime committed at La Criolla. It is rumored that one or more individuals from our select society could be connected to the tragic event. The police, provided with a search warrant, have searched the residence of a well-known attorney. It is alleged that said individual is a user of cocaine and other narcotics which, according to rumor, were obtained in establishments like La Criolla. All this suggests that the stains of Barcelona low-life are reaching into the city's best neighborhoods. Other headlines:* "*ECUADOR DAY IS CELEBRATED AT THE INTERNATIONAL EXPOSITION.*" "*Attendance by the illustrious ambassador of that republic.*" *An advertisement:* FRECKLE-FADER *(with the face of a young woman). News item:* "*Revival of* Die Götterdämmerung *at the Teatre del Liceu.*" *Another advertisement:* PALACE CINEMA, The Madonna of the Sleeping Cars. *Success of the year. Another advertisement:* BATACLAN TE-DANSANT. DEBUT OF THE INCOMPARABLE "FLOR DE OTOÑO." *Reserve your table now. An advertisement that ends the page:* WAGON LITS COOK. *While the newspaper fascimile is projected, we hear a melody, midway between sweet and trashy, abetted by a violin; and far in the distance the slow rhythm of a sardana. The page vanishes suddenly as if it had been torn away by the hand of an angry woman.*

After the newspaper disappears, we see **DOÑA NURIA** *dressed elegantly in a tailored suit and wearing a felt hat whose brim covers half her face (Pola Negri style).* **SHE** *is noisily hitting a Renaissance style office table with an umbrella. Behind the table, a* **YOUNG MAN** *who resembles Rudolph Valentino is trying to calm her. Seated in a small arm chair and looking remorseful is a thin, pale individual wearing glasses.* **HE** *is wrapped in a dark overcoat and seems utterly helpless.* **HE** *puts a handkerchief to his nose (apparently because he has a cold). Carpets, chandeliers, a large picture of Alfonso XIII. All of it tells us that we are in one of the offices of the municipal government.*

DOÑA NURIA: I want His Excellency to receive me. His Excellency, I said!
SECRETARY (*Stepping back a little from fear of getting struck by her umbrella*) : Impossible, señora, impossible. How many times do I have to tell you?
DOÑA NURIA: I am the widow of Don Lluís de Serracant!
SECRETARY: Yes, señora.
THE THIN YOUNG MAN (*Giggling*): Hee, hee . . .
DOÑA NURIA: Announce me . . . (*Saying this,* **SHE** *stands leaning on her umbrella like a queen on her staff of office.*)
SECRETARY: He's sick, I'm telling you. He has the flu.
DOÑA NURIA: He's going to have hemorrhoids! . . .
SECRETARY: Señora! . . . Señora! . . .
DOÑA NURIA: My name is Doña Nuria.
SECRETARY: Please, Doña Nuria, would you be so kind as to explain your complaint to me?
DOÑA NURIA: And just who are you?
SECRETARY: Señora, I am the secretary of the office of . . .
DOÑA NURIA: My good man, I don't know you.
SECRETARY: Pardon me, but . . .
DOÑA NURIA: I don't know what your name is. No one has ever introduced you to me. But I am . . .
SECRETARY: Yes, señora, Doña Nuria de Cañellas, widow of . . . .
DOÑA NURIA (*Now introducing her son*): And this gentleman, right there, is my son. My son and son of my husband, may he rest in peace. Lluís de Serracant, attorney at law, graduate with honors, a luminary of the courts. And this son of mine, I'll have you know, is not interested in politics, nor does getting ahead matter to him. Not like some others . . .
THE THIN YOUNG MAN: For heaven's sake, Mamá!
DOÑA NURIA: Just keep quiet! You still have someone who'll stand up for you. (*To the* **SECRETARY**) Do you hear that, sir? I am here to defend this gentleman, my son, whom all of you should be bowing to when he passes by. Don't speak! A model son, a model. A model citizen. And a model

Catalan, I'll have you know, you young whippersnapper . . . (*The SECRETARY tries to say something.*) No one, but no one, can say enough . . . (*SHE raises a clenched fist under the Secretary's nose and HE gives a frightened start.*) . . . about this gentleman in any matter: not his moral principles, nor his piety, nor his academic achievements. A mirror in which all those conspirators who try to belittle him should look at themselves. When they defame him, they defame me and, of course, my late husband and, therefore, my good man, they defame Catalunya. And injuring Catalunya they defame Spain . . .

THE THIN YOUNG MAN (*Standing up, HE attempts to restrain his mother, who is trying to strike the Secretary with the brandished umbrella.*): Mamá, Mamá, it's all right.

DOÑA NURIA: No, it isn't all right, it isn't! . . .

THE THIN YOUNG MAN (*In an affected but very firm voice*): In any case, my good man, it seems there's nothing more to be said. Just stop once and for all that injurious press campaign, end it right now! I am requesting it as a citizen and as the aggrieved party.

DOÑA NURIA (*Enraptured by the verbal display of her offspring*): Indeed! Indeed!

SECRETARY (*Bowing deeply as HE pushes a button on the desk*): I give you my word that I will transfer your complaint to the Governor. We are here to listen and serve you. (*An USHER appears at the door.*) Accompany the lady and the gentleman . . . Señora, señor . . .

DOÑA NURIA (*Very haughtily*): I kiss your hand, señor.

SECRETARY: I kiss your feet, señora.

DOÑA NURIA: But I don't know you. I don't know who you are. (*To her son as THEY exit.*) And you, Lluiset, do you know him? . . . (*THEY exit and the USHER bows. LIGHTS DOWN.*)

Family council at the home of the widow Serracant. A rainy afternoon. Gloomy darkness lit by the reflections from the fire in the fireplace and the lamp that hybrid child—half Cupid, half Mercury—holds aloft. Stiff figures seated in large armchairs. Pale and Judaic men. A fragile blond woman who stands out from the darkness of the others present. Another plump, ordinary-looking woman who keeps her hands out of sight in a muff. DOÑA NURIA presides over the meeting. SHE is still dressed in the tailored suit in the style of Pola Negri. More erect than any of the others, SHE lifts her Catalan matron's bust as if she were the incarnation of the ancient city. The shadow of the maid PILAR comes and goes, bringing tea cups and other things. THEY sit there rigid and silent. Over them hangs an accompaniment of operatic warbling that substitutes for words. THEY are all drinking coffee, almost in unison. There are many umbrellas about, some open, others closed, and from behind the bay window the rain dominates that funereal ceremony. *No one speaks. The warbling sounds increase until **DOÑA NURIA** takes the initiative.*

DOÑA NURIA: "You young whippersnapper, I don't know you, I don't know you, young man, I don't know your name," I told him. So I said to him, "really, now!"

A FAT, BALD GENTLEMAN: Ai, Deu Senyor! Heaven help us!

A GENTLEMAN THIN AS A SPATULA: Ai, carai! Goodness me!

DOÑA NURIA: "Really" I said. "Then would you be so kind as to . . ." I'd already said "please . . ."

A HUNCHBACKED GENTLEMAN (*Calling the servant*): Oh, Pilar, please bring me the little pills I left in my overcoat pocket . . .

(*Silence again.* **PILAR** *brings the pills and a glass of water.* **THE HUNCHBACKED GENTLEMAN** *dissolves one in water and then gargles in an operatic singsong.*)

DOÑA NURIA (*Breaking the silence again*): Then . . .
THE FAT GENTLEMAN: Then . . .
THE SKINNY GENTLEMAN: Then? . . .
THE HUNCHBACKED GENTLEMAN (*Clearing his throat*): Ai, Senyor!
DOÑA NURIA: Then . . . a Serracant, a true Serracant, has gotten mixed up with people from the underworld . . .
THE PLUMP LADY: Mare de Deu Santísima!
THE FAT GENTLEMAN: And it's quite clear then: Serracant Textiles is mixed up with the underworld.
THE BLOND LADY (*Starting to cry*): Oh my, I think I want to die . . . How will I ever set foot in the opera house again? Quina vergonya!
DOÑA NURIA: Politics has brought this on us.
THE SKINNY GENTLEMAN (*Raising a finger*): Politics, you've got it right . . . because it's obvious, politics is behind this.
THE HUNCHBACKED GENTLEMAN (*Able to talk after his coughing fit*): Envy, this is pure envy . . .
DOÑA NURIA: Oh, but it doesn't end there . . .
THE FAT GENTLEMAN: Indeed it doesn't!
THE SKINNY GENTLEMAN: Really? Then it would appear that Serracant Umbrellas, so respected since 1830, will be brought down by the misdeeds of a slanderer . . .
SEVERAL VOICES: Ai, Deu Senyor! Ai, Deu Senyor!
THE BLOND LADY: I've always said: tranquilitat i bons aliments . . .

DOÑA NURIA: And they say further that my son, that jewel, and a jewel he is, turns out to be a gunman, a cocaine addict, who associates with men in skirts.
THE HUNCHBACKED GENTLEMAN: What a fix!
DOÑA NURIA: Mare meva, when I was at my wits' end because he didn't want to get married and was already thirty years old! Trenta anys!
THE HUNCHBACKED GENTLEMAN: Oh, it's probably not because he doesn't want to. My Antonieta . . .
DOÑA NURIA (*Silencing him with a look*): This is not the moment for . . .
THE HUNCHBACKED GENTLEMAN: No, I was saying it because . . .
DOÑA NURIA (*Ignoring him*): And my son on the Paralelo. On the Paralelo.
THE PLUMP LADY: On the Paralelo . . .
DOÑA NURIA: Be quiet, since you yourself were seen once going to the Paralelo to see one of those scandalous revues.
THE PLUMP LADY: Then you were the one who saw me . . .
THE BLOND LADY (*To calm her down*): I've always said: rest and good nourishment . . . tranquilitat i bons aliments . . .
THE SKINNY GENTLEMAN: Or it may be that Lluiset, poor boy, is one of those "young barbarians" the politicians talk about.
THE BLOND LADY (*Crying again*): Ai, mare meva, what a disgrace!
THE FAT GENTLEMAN: Perhaps they should shut down the International Exposition as a precaution.
DOÑA NURIA (*Leaping up in fury*): What do you mean shut down? We Serracants will walk with our heads held high, no matter how much those determined liberals insult us . . . Mare meva, what am I saying?

(*Silence.*)

THE PLUMP LADY: And the fright that search must have given you, Nuria dear.
DOÑA NURIA: Indeed, but let Pilar tell you about it.
PILAR: Oh, what a scare, ma'am! . . . What a scare!

(*Another pause.*)

THE HUNCHBACKED GENTLEMAN: It's pure envy. Some wretch who doesn't like Lluiset, that's it.
DOÑA NURIA: And the business with the picture of Alfonso XIII, which the police themselves took away, let's say there was some politics involved.
THE PLUMP LADY: People are very bad, molt, molt dolenta.

THE BLOND LADY (*Who has stopped crying, has taken a mirror from her purse and is touching up her eyebrows*): And what are my friends going to say?

DOÑA NURIA: Well, we'll see who has the last laugh . . . ha, ha! . . .

(*Silence.*)

THE HUNCHBACKED GENTLEMAN: Well, then . . .

DOÑA NURIA: We'll defend ourselves, we'll defend ourselves tooth and nail. We'll fly our standard, in the place it's always been. What else?

THE PLUMP LADY: But I'm afraid . . . jo tinc por.

THE SKINNY GENTLEMAN: These are times of strife, times of strife. There's no law and order, no principles, so . . .

THE BLOND LADY: Ai, quina vergonya! And tomorrow I won't be able to go to the opera, and Toti dal Monte is singing . . . Oh my, oh my . . . (*We hear a dramatic roulade delivered with smug satisfaction.*)

THE HUNCHBACKED GENTLEMAN: That's the way things are going. All those Murcians from the South have come, there are a lot of bad folk in Barcelona, what with the Exposition and so many drugs. That's the problem. We're under siege . . .

DOÑA NURIA (*Raising herself up proudly*): Then let's defend ourselves!

ALL: Let's defend ourselves . . .

DOÑA NURIA (*Becoming more and more excited*): The son of Lluís de Serracant, intimate, most intimate friend of the Prime Minister. Lluís de Serracant, son in turn of that general . . . (*Points to the oil painting and all turn around to bow respectfully to it*) . . . who brought more glory to his country than General Prim himself, with a family dedicated to the most prosperous of businesses.

THE FAT GENTLEMAN: Serracant Textiles, I'll have you know . . .

THE SKINNY GENTLEMAN: Serracant Umbrellas . . .

THE HUNCHBACKED GENTLEMAN: Serracant Perfumes from Paris . . .

ALL: Ai, Deu Senyor! Heaven help us!

DOÑA NURIA: Ens defensarem!

THE HUNCHBACKED GENTLEMAN: We must devise a plan of action.

DOÑA NURIA: Oh, if his father were only living!

THE FAT GENTLEMAN: I'm a friend of the Finance Minister.

THE SKINNY GENTLEMAN: And I know the Minister of Public Works.

THE HUNCHBACKED GENTLEMAN: Well, I have a gangster friend who could . . .

(***THEY** all look horrified.*)

Autumn Flower-13

DOÑA NURIA What are you saying?
THE HUNCHBACKED GENTLEMAN: That is . . . I'll take another pill.
DOÑA NURIA: Dear me, now I see that I'm alone, with all of you at odds. Ai, Senyor, give me strength!
THE BLOND WOMAN: Oh, dear Nuria, we're all with you . . . Try to be calm.
THE HUNCHBACKED GENTLEMAN: And try to get good nourishment, bons aliments.
THE FAT GENTLEMAN: And keep your head up . . .
DOÑA NURIA (*Getting up*): Well then, now you know everything.

*And with this "Now you know everything," **DOÑA NURIA** terminates the family council.* ***THEY*** *all stand and begin their very drawn out, ritualized goodbyes. But we only see their gestures as they debate—whatever such people debate— put on their overcoats and take their umbrellas. A scene of shadowy marionettes. Meanwhile, the lights have come up on a corner of the stage and we see **LLUISET**—that is, the dear child who has produced such a moral earthquake.* ***HE*** *is in a kind of bachelor's apartment carpeted in red. His glasses lie on a small table.* ***LLUISET*** *appears to us now very different from the way we saw him at the interview with the secretary of the municipal office. Dressed in pants, cummerbund, and tuxedo jacket, with his glasses off, he looks like a gay gigolo.* ***HE*** *is looking at himself in the mirror, smoothing back his hair and applying pomade. We notice that he is taking time grooming himself.* ***HE*** *uses atomizers, colognes, and a thousand other trifles. While he is fixing up,* ***HE*** *whistles happily. Meanwhile, we continue to see upstage the family group miming their drawn out goodbyes.* ***LLUISET*** *steps back from the mirror to admire himself.* ***HE*** *clicks his heels rhythmically, places his hands on his hips, and walks toward the mirror vamp-like in the manner of Mae West. Suddenly, as if remembering something,* ***HE*** *goes to the telephone, which is on a small table, and dials a number.* ***HE*** *taps the floor nervously with his foot, with an even, coquettish movement.*

LLUISET: Hello? . . . Señorita . . . señorita. What about my call to Vilanova? Not yet? Half an hour? By your time or mine, dear? Now don't be that way, sweet . . . Take pity on a man who's in love. (*Emphasizing*) A man in love. (*With a girlish cry*) Ooooh! Really! How did you know it? Honest to goodness? Cross your heart? . . . (*Kissing the receiver*) I'm sending you a kiss, and another. Bless you and your mother, too, you brazen girl . . . Olé!

(*HE hangs up, does a few dance steps, and returns to the mirror. Then HE takes down a cape and holds it crosswise, flamenco style, and marches across the stage like a flamenco cabaret singer. HE takes a flower from a bouquet and places it over his ear. HE looks at himself, doesn't like the look, and removes the flower. In the shadows his relatives begin the rite of kisses and embraces. Now the telephone rings and LLUISET runs toward it, tossing the cape aside. HE answers the phone nervously.*)

Hello? Hello? Vilanova? . . . Vilanova? What's that? I can't hear you at all. Listen, senyoreta, senyoreta! . . . Yes, yes, I'm here. Ja estic, dona. Vilanova . . . Is it Vilanova? (*Angry, HE kicks the cape, which had fallen at his feet.*) Ricard! . . . Ricard! . . . Is it you? . . . Is it Ricard? Listen. What? What did you say? Pepe? No, no, it's the wrong number. I asked for Ricard . . . I don't need any Pepes. Well, really! (*HE hangs up in anger and dials again.*) Senyoreta, senyoreta . . . I got a wrong number, I got someone named Pepe and it's a name I don't like . . . What did you say, dear? No, no. Ricard in Vilanova. Not Pepe in Valbona . . . Come now! You say you're having a bad day? Yes, well it's probably because of the weather . . . Fine. I'll wait for you, biting my nails. (*HE hangs up and crosses his arms. HE looks at his wristwatch.*) Some telephone system! (*Another ring. HE picks up quickly.*) Hello . . . yes, yes. Is that you Ricard? It's about time! . . . You've had me beside the phone all evening, my love. Where were you? At that bar? You devil . . . you little scamp. I don't believe you. What I've been through! You know all about it? Oh, you do. I should have guessed you would. You're a real Sherlock Holmes. (*With a little cry*) Imagine, imagine. What a scandal! The works, the works. Search by the police, the police station, heaven help me. They went to the house . . . Who me? Calm as can be . . . What? I can't hear you . . . Oh, yes. Tonight. I'll wait for you. I'll tell you all the details. Everything, everything, of course. Have I ever had secrets from you, dear boy? Try to come early. In the private room, yes. Will you come in Surroca's Rolls? Oh, how exciting . . . you'll see . . . Goodbye, handsome. Petons, molts petons. A thousand kisses. Hurry up! Bye, now. Au revoir! (*HE hangs up with a sigh of satisfaction and dials again.*) Senyoreta, there you are. Oh my, you have no idea, no idea. Many thanks, you pretty thing. Adéu. And good luck to you with all those men with bedroom eyes . . . (*Hangs up*).

(*HE runs through the room happily. The silhouettes of his relatives are still dancing in the shadows. HE puts on a bow tie, throws the cape over this tuxedo jacket, and puts on a top hat at an angle. HE picks up a thin cane and now he is a figure from a sleazy cabaret with Parisian pretentions. HE twirls the cane in front of the mirror, and the mirror gives him back his raffish figure, with plucked eyebrows and eyes made up with eyeshadow.* **HE** *walks upstage, takes out a handkerchief and waves at his relatives who are now filing out like figures from a wake and daubing their eyes with their handkerchiefs. From offstage, we hear Lluiset's high pitched voice as if recorded on a 78rpm record.* **HE** *is singing a number that begins like this:*)

Flower of the cabaret . . .
with sultry eyes that lead astray,
A hothouse flower from Paris.
They call me "Flor de Otoño,
exotic autumn flower from Paris.

(*And with the last verse from the scratchy record, the stage becomes totally dark.*)

Shining, flickering lights full of restlessness and longing announce: **BATACLAN. TE DANSANT. DEBUT: FLOR DE OTOÑO, THE AUTUMN FLOWER.** *The mad night along the Barcelona boulevard known as the Paralelo in the 1930s. A varied crowd made up of vagrants, Bohemians, hustlers, camouflaged individuals from good society, foreigners visiting the city for the International Exposition, anarchists, gamblers. A din of horse-drawn carriages, Berlins, and automobiles. At the door of the Bataclan Cabaret a girl is singing the famous copla "Baixant de la Font del Gat." A January night with the scent of mimosa. In the vestibule of the Bataclan, red velvet curtains conceal the sinful goings-on. Esoteric photographs. Harsh, aggressive light.* **THE CLOAKROOM ATTENDANT** *bleached blond and almost a sexagenarian, a kind of pythoness who opens the way of mysteries and smiles malevolently as she counsels the hesitant ones. Stationed at the door,* **THE DOORMAN,** *in a braided uniform, visored cap, enormous sideburns, presents to us a working man from the Born Market district who is moonlighting. It is debut night and among the habitual clientele we see some ladies who are returning from the opera and are oblivious to the dangers to which their ermine capes, mink stoles, and jewels expose them. They are delighted to see themselves mingling with the flower of the underworld. All sorts of murmurs and excitement resulting from the news stories. There is a couple looking at the photographs outside.* **SHE** *looks like a modiste in her best dress and* **HE** *is a young madcap from a good family.*

THE GIRL: Look, that's her. They say she cut La Asturianita to pieces . . .
THE GUY: So she wouldn't be outshone.

THE GIRL: It's exciting. Can we go in?
THE GUY (*Very suggestive*): I can tell the sort of things you like.
THE GIRL: Come on, don't be naughty . . . (*THEY disappear through the curtains.*)
DOORMAN (*To the CLOAKROOM ATTENDANT*): What a crowd! It's going to get crazy here tonight, Montse.
CLOAKROOM ATTENDANT: Have the cops come?
DOORMAN (*Fixated*): Tonight'll be good. I tell you, one hell of a show.
CLOAKROOM ATTENDANT: For me it's a bore!

(*At this moment, a fellow with the air of a Chicago gangster mixed with a classic small-town business man from Murcia appears in the vestibule. A stocky, hairy monster who creates quite an impression. His clothes which aim to be elegant—overcoat with astrakhan collar, contribute to making him all the more unsettling. With him are two guys who make a show of their function as body guards. This character is known as "**THE WIDOWER OF LA ASTURIANITA.**" THE DOORMAN, on seeing him, confronts him courageously.*)

DOORMAN: I'm sorry, gentlemen. The house is full. Tot ple . . .
WIDOWER: What are you telling me, you . . . ?
DOORMAN (*Giving the monster a part on the back*): We've reached the limit. God and his mother too have come here tonight. It's packed to the rafters.
WIDOWER (*Brushing him aside politely but firmly*): Let me go in . . .
DOORMAN (*Frightened*): But the house is full! There's another show tomorrow and besides . . .
BODYGUARD (*To the DOORMAN*): Go back to the farm!

(*And the three sinister characters slip by. The CLOAKROOM ATTENDANT puts up one last obstacle*)

CLOAKROOM ATTENDANT: Sirs? Your coats? . . .
BODYGUARD: Here, and shut up! (*HE tosses her a coin.*)
DOORMAN (*Taking off his cap and scratching his head.*): Oh, boy! Now we're in for it. That guy is . . . (*Lowers his voice*).
CLOAKROOM ATTENDANT: Mare meva santísima! We'd better call the cops. I'll get Senyor Barral . . .
DOORMAN: I did all I could, but they're gangsters . . .

(*At this moment, the kind of Rolls Royce that always transports big stars pulls up at the door. People crowd around. The famous star **FLOR DE OTOÑO** is arriving with that friend of hers, **RICARD**; and at the wheel is an*

Félix Martin as Lluiset, Flor de Otoño.
Production by Les Anachroniques, Toulouse, France, 1992.
Photo courtesy of José María Rodríguez Méndez.

*ex-boxer, with anarchist sympathies, who is called **EL SURROCA**. The hoi polloi hanging out at the door applaud. **FLOR DE OTOÑO**, or rather, **LLUISET**, is radiantly happy under the diabolic light of the twinkling sign. **HE** takes off his top hat and greets them.*)

A GIRL: How lovely!
A WOMAN: Look at those eyes!
A MAN (*To the **WOMAN***): It's all phoney.
THE WOMAN: That's what you think!
DOORMAN (*To **FLOR DE OTOÑO** as he gets out of the car*): Do you know who's come, dear?
LLUISET: Who, sweetheart? (*The **DOORMAN** whispers something in his ear.*) So what? Is that why you're shouting?
DOORMAN: It's just that he came with two of his . . .
RICARD: What did he say?
LLUISET: Nothing. That one of the low-life is here.
EL SURROCA: That's why they reserve the right of admission.
CLOAKROOM ATTENDANT (*To **LLUISET***): Oh, Flor, you're getting here a bit late, darling . . .
LLUISET (*Kissing the **CLOAKROOM ATTENDANT** coquetishly*): Muu . . . muu . . . I never arrive late; quite the contrary; exactly on time, a punt.
CLOAKROOM ATTENDANT: Do you know who's here?
LLUISET: A lot of admirers . . . molts admiradors.
CLOAKROOM ATTENDANT: I hope nothing happens to you . . .

(*Laughing, **THEY** leave their coats and disappear behind the curtains. The **DOORMAN** takes off his cap again.*)

DOORMAN: Right now is when I'd like to see some of the guys I work with show up.
CLOAKROOM ATTENDANT: Oh, you people . . . this is what the cops are for.
DOORMAN: But you heard how I spoke to him.
CLOAKROOM ATTENDANT: How you spoke to him? Hah!
DOORMAN: Goddamn it! What did you expect me to do with those two others with him?
CLOAKROOM ATTENDANT: It's all the same to me.
DOORMAN (*To a couple who are about to enter*): Senyor? . . .

(*The couple are the **HUNCHBACKED GENTLEMAN** we saw at Doña Nuria's family council and a **CHORUS GIRL** from the Sugranyes Theatre Company.*)

HUNCHBACKED GENTLEMAN: We'd like to go in to the debut of the incomparable Flor de Otoño.
DOORMAN: I'm sorry, senyor, but the house is full.
CHORUS GIRL: Full? Oh! . . .
HUNCHBACKED GENTLEMAN: Don't worry, nena . . . Listen, young man, ascolti . . .
DOORMAN: We're full, senyor, sold out.
HUNCHBACKED GENTLEMAN: Do you know who I am? . . .
DOORMAN: I haven't had the pleasure, senyor, but we're full up.
HUNCHBACKED GENTLEMAN: I'll have you know I'm a partner in this enterprise.
DOORMAN: No, I didn't know, senyor, but I have my orders.
HUNCHBACKED GENTLEMAN: Come now, don't be so tiresome, don't make things difficult. We want a good table . . .
DOORMAN: The hell you say! If I tell you there's nothing, then there's nothing . . . If you are one of the partners, speak with Senyor Barral.
CHORUS GIRL: You aren't being very nice to us.
DOORMAN: I have my orders.
CHORUS GIRL (*Pressing the Hunchbacked Gentleman's arm with her jewelled little hand*): I do so want to go in . . .
HUNCHBACKED GENTLEMAN (*Trying to bribe the DOORMAN*): Here, take this and look the other way . . .
DOORMAN (*Looking at the bills the HUNCHBACKED GENTLEMAN is trying to give him*): Damn it to hell, didn't I tell you no?
HUNCHBACKED GENTLEMAN: And don't you know who I am? Huh?
DOORMAN: All right, then, fellow . . . (*And HE takes the old man by the neck, turns him around, and shoves him into the street. The CHORUS GIRL screams.*)
CHORUS GIRL: You big lout! You thug!
DOORMAN (*Wiping off his hands*): I've had enough of your stories.
CLOAKROOM ATTENDANT: That old guy's saying something . . .
DOORMAN: He acts like he's the Pope, so what's it to me?

(*At this moment* **THREE MEN** *enter and show their badges. The* **DOORMAN** *takes off his cap and greets them.* **THEY** *go inside.*)

DOORMAN (*Pleased*): Now we've got some protection. We can take it easier.

(*A salvo of applause from inside and the lights go down.*)

Now we have the famous star **FLOR DE OTOÑO** on stage. *Dressed in pants, shirt and bow tie of the tuxedo, but the jacket has been exchanged for a sequined coat. A multicolored feather on the top hat. His eyes are made up, and his lips painted in the shape of a small heart. His face is a slightly oriental mask. A burst of applause greets his entrance. There is a gasp of satisfaction from a public that appears in the shadows.* **FLOR DE OTOÑO**, *twirling a cane, reminds us of a mysterious and haughty Marlene Dietrich.* **HE** *sings with a raspy voice like that of "Bella Dorita" and moves with the worldly air of a showy vamp.*

FLOR DE OTOÑO (*Singing*):

> Flower of the cabaret
> with sultry eyes that lead astray
> A hothouse flower from Paris.
> They call me "Flor de Otoño,"
> exotic import from Paris.

A VOICE FROM THE AUDIENCE: You're one hell of a girl, nena.
ANOTHER VOICE: The best sight in Barcelona.
FLOR DE OTOÑO (*Beginning to stroll among the tables, singing in a soft voice and ignoring the noise-makers*)**:**

> With a gift that brings delight
> when sniffed all through the night,
> co, co, co, cocaine . . . Oh, my!

(**HE** *stops, surveys the public, and sighs.*)

ONE OF THE AUDIENCE: Come over here and turn me on.
ANOTHER VOICE: I've got some cocaine you can sniff, nena.
AN ANGRY VOICE: Shut up, you shit heads! . . .
FLOR DE OTOÑO (*Unperturbed*):

> Just give me your hand
> And I will understand . . .
> You'll share my co, co, cocaine.

(*The spots now light the tables, and* **FLOR DE OTOÑO** *has done nothing less than take the hand of the terrible* **WIDOWER OF LA ASTURIANITA**, *who was his rival. The monster frowns. At the opposite table we see the* *friends of the artist—**RICARD** and **EL SURROCA**—on their guard. In the background the silhouettes of the cops.)*

FLOR DE OTOÑO (*Caressing the hand of the **WIDOWER** *): Oh my, such hands, these are what I call hands, and I should know! (***HE*** *tries to raise the hand to his face, and the monster pulls it away brusquely as he says something unintelligible.* ***FLOR DE OTOÑO*** *laughs.*) Ooooh . . . What a temper! That's the way I like my men with a temper, the way men should be, just like they are in the theatre. It brings out my gypsy blood, even though I was born in Paris. (*Singing and moving away from the unfriendly table.*)

Ah, yes, Paris, Paris . . .
Hothouse flower from old Paris . . .

(*Stopping and reciting*) Paris, oh Paris . . . But what can compare with beautiful Barcelona and all those fountains and flowers. Obviously, I can't. Who would notice me, one autumn flower, amid a sea of blossoms? Let's take a look as some who are right here in the Bataclan Cabaret. (*The spotlight moves across the heads of several ladies.*) Oh, spare me! They can't compare with Chez Maxim. So you won't deny that I'm "la flor de las flores," "flor florum," as they say in Latin. You see, I'm an educated girl, too . . . Oooh, handsome! . . . (***HE*** *has tweaked Ricard's nose and returns to the center of the floor singing anew.*)

Give me, give me, give me, a whiff
of your co, co, co, cocaine . . . oh, please.

WIDOWER (*To the others at the table*): If she tries to make a fool of me again, I'll give her something she won't forget . . .
ONE OF THE BODYGUARDS: Not yet, not yet . . .
FLOR DE OTOÑO (*Wiggling his hips*):

For I'm a hothouse flower,
An autumn flower from afar,
A rose from China or Dakar . . .
(*Reciting*) Come on, everybody, sing with me. Be daring!

(*Laughter, cheers, and applause, and a raucous chorus that tries to accompany the vedette.*)

22 - José María Rodríguez Méndez

CHORUS:

> An autumn flower from afar,
> A rose from China or Dakar,
> Chiiina, or Dakaaar . . .

(**FLOR DE OTOÑO** *stops at the table of a man with the look of a American financier, who is accompanied by two upper-crust ladies. Very suggestive, speaking the words:*)

> Come on, don't be that way,
> Share your co, co, cocaine with me.
> You've charmed me, can't you see?

(*Now singing*)
> You look at me and I feel faint,
> I need a whiff so desperately,
> so share with me your co, co, cocaine . . .

(*Stopping and speaking*) Do you know what happened to me the other day on the Rambla? Well, you know what it's like these days on the Rambla. Oh my, yes! You can't take a step without attracting attention. With all those foreigners. With the smell of men everywhere. And all those swells! What can a girl do, I ask you. I don't want to sound immodest, but a girl can't take a quiet stroll on the Rambla anymore. The other day they wrapped me in paper and carried me before His Majesty, who had asked them to bring him the most beautiful flower from the Rambla . . . Ooooh!

(*A commotion breaks out. The people stamp their feet. It sounds like a zoo, and* **FLOR DE OTOÑO,** *swaying his hips, returns to the center of the floor, raises his cane, takes a few dance steps, and goes through the motions of directing the chorus, moving his hips with outrageous abandon.*)
> I'm a hothouse flower from afar,
> A rose from China or Dakar . . .

Come on, come on, everybody!

CHORUS:

> An autumn flower from afar,
> A rose from China or Dakar.
> From Chiiina, or Dakaaar . . .

FLOR DE OTOÑO:

A rare exotic flower,
my eyes speak of desire.
So let me share your passion
And I'll give you . . .

(*Asking*)

What will I give you?
Something very nice . . .
Cocaine, cocaaaine . . .

(*The spotlight has been focussed on the star as* **HE** *was singing the verses, and a burst of thundering applause follows. The star bows, throwing kisses with his delicate hand.* **HE** *exits and reenters.* **HE** *is radiant. His triumph has been complete. When the applause dies down, the lights come up in the cabaret and* **FLOR DE OTOÑO** *starts toward his friends' table, ignoring the compliments that come from other tables.* **RICARD** *kisses Flor de Otoño's hand and* **SURROCA** *does the same.* **HE** *sits down with them while keeping his eye on the table of his rivals—that is, Asturianita's* **WIDOWER** *and his chums.*)

RICARD: You were fabulous, nena.
SURROCA: Colossal, beautiful . . .
FLOR DE OTOÑO: Did you see how I stood up to them?
RICARD: Donc, ascolta, nena. Don't do anything silly. The cops are here.
SURROCA: And some guy from the Free Workers' Union.
FLOR DE OTOÑO (*Very showy*): Well, they can all search me . . .

(*Couples begin to dance on the dance floor.* **FLOR DE OTOÑO** *lights a long Turkish cigarette which* **HE** *offers to his friend Ricard.*)

RICARD: Don't do anything rash, there's still a lot to be done.
FLOR DE OTOÑO: The night's young . . . (*Calling the waiter*) Garçon, garçon! . . .
WAITER (*Coming over*): What would you like, treasure of the house?
FLOR DE OTOÑO: Tell those guys . . . (*Pointing to the* **WIDOWER'S** *table*)
. . . that I'm inviting them for drinks. The poor things look so thirsty.
WAITER (*Stepping away with a laugh*): Get her!
RICARD: Don't do anything crazy, nena . . .

FLOR DE OTOÑO: I'll do what I feel like doing. It's my debut, smart ass. So be nice to me.

(*The WAITER slips through the couples who are dancing with a slow rhythm and stops before the WIDOWER'S table.*)

WAITER: The star of the evening would like to know what you're drinking, she's inviting you . . .
WIDOWER: Tell her we're not her pimps.
WAITER: Listen, I'm only delivering her message . . .
A BODYGUARD: Then shit on the messenger.

(*At that point, FLOR DE OTOÑO rushes toward the WIDOWER'S table, evading the friends who try to stop him.*)

FLOR DE OTOÑO (*Smartly, with hands on hips*)**:** What's new in Cádiz?

(*The WIDOWER is as motionless as an Egyptian mummy.*)

A BODYGUARD: Up your ass, sweety!
FLOR DE OTOÑO: Oh, how exciting!
WAITER: I've done my duty. (*HE leaves to serve another table.*)
FLOR DE OTOÑO (*Taking the WIDOWER'S hand*)**:** Will you dance with me, grumpy? (*No answer*) It's our tango . . .
WIDOWER: Do you know who I am?
FLOR DE OTOÑO: A man . . . what I'm looking for.
WIDOWER: Do you know why I came tonight?
FLOR DE OTOÑO: To steal hearts, dark and handsome.
WIDOWER: To avenge someone you used to know . . .
FLOR DE OTOÑO: Oh, don't talk about sad things now. La Asturianita was the jewel of my eye. Everyone will tell you that. Why, this very day I sent a wreath.
WIDOWER: Look, the cops are here, and I don't need any trouble.
FLOR DE OTOÑO: But, silly, why worry? Forget it with me, adorable. Come on, the tango's beginning. I'll tell you some things about your Asturianita . . .

(*The WIDOWER gets up and goes onto the dance floor with FLOR DE OTOÑO. At the table of the others*)

SURROCA: That whore's picked him up.
RICARD: Get yourself ready.

SURROCA: I am ready, but that slut's going to get you into big trouble.
RICARD: I didn't stop her and I can't leave her stranded now.
SURROCA: I can't believe you have a heart for this sort of thing. Me either. Too much time spent correcting poets' galleys has made me sentimental.
A MAN (*Getting up from a table and running toward the police*): My wallet! They've lifted my wallet! They've lifted it!
ANOTHER MAN: Big news! Who would have thought of that?

(*On the dance floor, a spot on* **FLOR DE OTOÑO** *and the* **WIDOWER**.)

FLOR DE OTOÑO: Did you love her a lot?
WIDOWER (*In a cavernous voice*): Who?
FLOR DE OTOÑO: Who do you think? Your Asturianita! . . .
WIDOWER: If you mention her again, I'll strangle you . . .

(*In effect* **HE** *places his large hands around* **FLOR DE OTOÑO'S** *neck.*)

FLOR DE OTOÑO (*Laughing nervously*): Ooooh, what a touch·you have! What strong hands! Do you work on the docks, handsome?
WIDOWER: I'm a man of my word, and if I knew for sure that you were . . .
FLOR DE OTOÑO (*Removing the hands from his neck*): That I was what?
WIDOWER: The one who murdered my goddess.
FLOR DE OTOÑO: Oh, my goddess! How you talk. You're a poet . . .
WIDOWER: You bitch, I'll strangle you . . .

(*At that moment,* **RICARD** *is beside them.*)

RICARD: Our dance, nena.
WIDOWER (*Ignoring him*): It's going to be a great night.
FLOR DE OTOÑO: A night on the Paralelo.
RICARD (*Slapping the* **WIDOWER** *on the shoulder*): Hey, friend . . .
WIDOWER (*Turning around*): Who are you calling friend?
RICARD (*Very annoyed, to* **FLOR**): All right, beautiful . . .

(*At the moment* **HE** *starts to take* **FLOR DE OTOÑO** *by the waist, the* **WIDOWER** *rushes at him and butts him hard in the stomach with his head.* **RICARD** *crumples to the floor. A big scream from* **FLOR** *and a general uproar. The* **COPS** *step forward.* **SURROCA** *takes out a pistol. The Widower's* **BODYGUARDS** *go to his aid. As* **RICARD** *is getting up, the* **WIDOWER** *has pulled out an enormous knife and attacks* **FLOR DE OTOÑO**, *giving him a slash on the neck. Horrified screams from the* onlookers. **SURROCA** *fires at the* **WIDOWER**. *The* **POLICE** *fire in the air. The music continues playing as the LIGHTS COME DOWN.*)

The ATARAZANAS MILITARY BARRACKS at the edge of the harbor. **HOOKERS** *lurking in the corners in expectation of some raw recruit eager to get it off. The wee hours of the morning. The sound of cranes from the nearby port. The lit statue of Columbus standing like a beacon. The* **SENTRY** *on duty passes by making his rounds and the vague shapes of the hookers slip away. Suddenly a group arrives running.* **RICARD** *and* **SURROCA** *are carrying* **FLOR DE OTOÑO** *seated on their clasped arms. His head falls to one side like a camellia blossom.* **HE** *tries to stanch the bleeding with his hands.*

FLOR DE OTOÑO: Help, I'm bleeding to death! My blood's draining out of me! I'm Marguerite Gautier . . .
RICARD: Damn it to hell! Just shut up!
SURROCA: I think we've given them the slip. What do we do now?
FLOR DE OTOÑO: What do we do now? Get help! (*Screaming*) Help, guards, please . . . help me, I'm dyyying! . . .

(*The* **HOOKERS** *reappear in the shadows.*)

FIRST HOOKER: Who's screaming?
SECOND HOOKER: One of the girls must have got bumped off.
FIRST HOOKER: Men are all brutes.
FLOR DE OTOÑO: Help! . . . Guards! . . .
RICARD: Will you just shut up? Do you want to get us all into big trouble?
FLOR DE OTOÑO: It doesn't matter as long as I see that evil-minded man, who threw me in the gutter, hanging from a gallows!
SURROCA: Oh, goddamn!

(*The guard detachment on duty approaches. Four sleepy-eyed* **RECRUITS** *and a* **CORPORAL**.)

CORPORAL: Halt! Who goes there?
RICARD (*Shouting*): Please, it's a wounded man.
FLOR DE OTOÑO: No, no. Say: It's the Queen of Spain . . .
CORPORAL (*Badhumoredly*): Like hell! Just who are you?
FLOR DE OTOÑO (*In a sweet voice*): The Queen of Spaaiin . . .
RICARD (*Loudly*): Gent de pau . . . peaceful people.

(*The* **RECRUITS** *crouch in the shadows.*)

A RECRUIT: Don't listen to them, corporal. They're whores.
CORPORAL (*With a dance of pleasure*): Yeah, yeah!
ANOTHER RECRUIT: And there're some thugs with the whores.
CORPORAL (*Stepping forward*): Which of you says she's the Queen of Spain?

(*FLOR DE OTOÑO appears beautifully bloodied; and behind, in the shadows, we can make out the outlines of his chums.*)

FLOR DE OTOÑO: Captain, captain, captain of the Flemish Regiment . . .
CORPORAL: Oh, man! This gal is really sloshed.
FLOR DE OTOÑO: I'm mortally wounded . . . aaaahh!
CORPORAL: Oh, shit . . . that's some gash you got! And, hey, you look like a guy . . .
FLOR DE OTOÑO: I'm really the Marqués de la Marina. I've just been assaulted . . . aaaahh! (*HE coughs up blood.*)
RICARD (*Coming forward*): They attacked us when we were coming out of the Bataclan Cabaret. They slashed the Marqués. Didn't you hear shots?
CORPORAL: So what's new? Fuck off! This is a matter for the cops.
FLOR DE OTOÑO: You're going to let me bleed to death?
CORPORAL: This is a military post.
SURROCA: You're not going to refuse someone help . . .
A HOOKER (*Who has come up close to look*): It's a young man. He's cute, too, if you don't mind me saying it. And stabbed like a pig.
FLOR DE OTOÑO: I'll die in the heart of the Barrio Chino. In the middle of the underworld. What better death can befall a Barcelona aristocrat?
CORPORAL: Cut the shit! . . .
A RECRUIT: God forgive me, but the Marqués looks like a queer to me.
SURROCA: Come on now, Corporal. Have them open the gate to help a gentleman.
CORPORAL: I don't have any orders to do that, my friend.
RICARD: When your superior the Captain General finds out tomorrow, we'll see what happens. I have dinner with him every evening . . .
FLOR DE OTOÑO: With Anastasio? He would die if he saw me in this mess! Such a death! I'm so like La Traviata . . .
CORPORAL (*Doubtful*): The most I can do is inform the officer in charge.
RECRUIT: He's probably dead to the world. And if you wake him up . . .
CORPORAL (*To the RECRUIT*): You go wake him up and tell him what's happened.
RECRUIT: Hell no! He'll skin me alive if I do that . . .
CORPORAL: And I'll do worse if you don't, so go!

FLOR DE OTOÑO (*Seeing the young soldier running toward the door*): Not so fast, little boy, or you'll fall and break your neck and we'll end up lovers in heaven.

RICARD: Will you cut it out? You're making me nervous.

SURROCA (*By way of explanation to the **SERGEANT***): It's just a matter of letting him rest a bit inside and getting emergency treatment.

RICARD: Basic human kindness . . .

CORPORAL: If you were all at home and not hanging out in the wrong places at this hour, nothing serious would have happened to you.

FLOR DE OTOÑO: The night casts its spells . . .

(*The main door opens and the substantial silhouette of the **LIEUTENANT** of the Guard appears. **HE** is leaning on his sword like Jupiter on his lightning bolt.*)

LIEUTENANT: What's going on?

CORPORAL: At your orders, sir. Nothing special . . .

FLOR DE OTOÑO (*Reacting excitedly*): What do you mean nothing special? Really! Here I am bleeding to death and it's nothing special?

RICARD (*To the **LIEUTENANT***): Robbers. They attacked us when we were coming home from the Exposition . . .

LIEUTENANT: I'm sorry, but . . .

CORPORAL (*Drawing him aside a little*): They seem to be important people.

LIEUTENANT: I don't want any problems.

SURROCA: Listen, my friend, we only need a little first aid. The Marqués is dying . . .

RICARD: Nothing more than basic human kindness.

FLOR DE OTOÑO: Aaahh, now that I'm in the arms of the Spanish army I can die in peace.

LIEUTENANT: What's he talking about?

RICARD: The poor boy's delirious.

LIEUTENANT: Take him inside and go get someone to treat him.

FLOR DE OTOÑO: I knew that a proud officer wouldn't let me die in the gutter . . .

LIEUTENANT: Yeah, well you all look soused to me. Rich guys out on the town, fuck you all!

(***RICARD** and **SURROCA** carry **FLOR DE OTOÑO** into the guard house, while the **LIEUTENANT** swings his saber in the Mediterranean night.*)

LIEUTENANT: But he's right. An officer can't deny help to a person in need. The bad part's having to write up a report. And I was dead to the world.

(*Inside the guardhouse. Dark vaults.* **THEY** *leave the fair* **FLOR**, *jacket bloodied, brilliantined hair mussed, on a table. The* **RECRUITS** *come up to watch.*)

CORPORAL (*To the* **SOLDIERS**): Get the hell away and give him some air!
A RECRUIT: Just a little more and they'd have slit his gullet . . .
ANOTHER RECRUIT: They knew just where to put the blade.
FLOR DE OTOÑO: Am I in heaven? Oh, what lovely company! Now I really am La Traviata . . .

(*Laughs from the* **RECRUITS.**)

A RECRUIT: He's a queer, alright.
CORPORAL: Get out of here, damn it, or you're all going to be sorry!

(*The* **LIEUTENANT** *enters.*)

LIEUTENANT: Go get a medic, and step on it. Have them treat him and get them out of here. Call the sergeant so he can make a report . . .

(**FLOR DE OTOÑO** *is now lying on the table and a couple of the* **RECRUITS** *take him by the hand.* **HE** *is humming fragments of Verdi's* La Traviata.)

LIEUTENANT: Drunk too?
RICARD: You know how a person of this sort always has to live it up a bit. Four small drinks did it.
LIEUTENANT: I wasn't blaming him.
FLOR DE OTOÑO (*Sitting up and fixing his eyes on the* **LIEUTENANT**): What a man! The Cid himself. I'm your Jimena. Put me on your steed Babieca and let us flee through the orchards of Valencia . . .
LIEUTENANT (*Stepping back. Laughter from the* **SOLDIERS**): Damn, he's really sloshed.
RICARD: The fever makes him that way.
LIEUTENANT: I don't know who he takes me for . . .
FLOR DE OTOÑO: For the flower of knighthood. I am Dulcinea . . .
LIEUTENENT: My God, I think he really is a queer.

(*Now a sleepy-eyed* **SOLDIER** *arrives with a first aid kit in his hand.*}

MEDIC (*Pronouncing "s" with an Andalusian lisp*): At your orders, sir . . . where's the wounded guy?
LIEUTENANT (*To the **SOLDIERS** and threatening them with his saber*): Get back or I'll crack your heads open. (*To the **MEDIC***) There's the guy, or whatever he is. Give him first aid and get him out of here.
RICARD (*To the **LIEUTENANT** while the **MEDIC** attends to **FLOR DE OTOÑO***): We won't forget your noble act. Who knows, maybe you'll be recommended for a promotion.
LIEUTENANT (*With false modesty*): I'm not a person who expects honors. Especially in these times . . .
SURROCA: It's obvious that you're a true man of the uniform.
LIEUTENANT: Just a soldier . . . (***HE** breaks off the sentence and steps back as **HE** adds.*) Take all the time you need. There's plenty of security here. This is no time of the night to be risking your hides . . .
RICARD: I don't know how I can thank you on behalf of the Marqués.

(*The **LIEUTENANT** exits. The **MEDIC** examines Flor de Otoño's wound.*)

MEDIC: Mi mare! That's some cut you've got! Who did it to you?
FLOR DE OTOÑO: Some wicked man who wanted to steal my necklace. And he did. But as a reward I find myself in your hands . . . (***HE** kisses them.*) Which are worth more than the diamonds the Shah of Persia gave me.
MEDIC (*Taking his hands away with amusement*): What are you talking about? Hey, you're too much . . .
FLOR DE OTOÑO: You're my sultan now, and I'm the favorite in your harem.
MEDIC (*Half aside*): A raving fag . . . Well, you're going to need a few stitches. But I have to stop the bleeding first.

(*Meanwhile, **RICARD** and **SURROCA**, taking advantage of the Lieutenant's absence, go over to the gun rack where the rifles are stored. The **SOLDIERS** have already snuggled into their capes and are dozing in the vaulted shadows.*)

RICARD (*Giving the guns the once over*): Mauser rifles from the Cuba campaign.
SURROCA: They could be useful . . . (*Grabbing a rifle.*) And this one's loaded.
RICARD: They're made in America.
SURROCA (*Hiding a rifle under his coat*): A memento.
RICARD (*A bit scandalized*): You're going to take it with you?
SURROCA: Let's make hay while the sun shines.

Autumn Flower-31

RICARD (*Handing him another rifle*): Take another one, you've got room.
SURROCA: Let's see. (*Takes a few steps.*) It's just a matter of arranging my appearance.
RICARD: You certainly look sturdy.

(***SURROCA** goes toward the door with the two concealed rifles.*)

SURROCA: I'll go find a cab. To move our wounded friend . . .
RICARD: Yes, we've already abused the hospitablity of these gentlemen enough.

(***SURROCA** exits.*)

FLOR DE OTOÑO: I'm dying, I'm fading fast! Just like La Traviata. La Traviata. Did you know, dear boy, that I've led a sinful life? And now I'm repenting . . .
MEDIC (*As **HE** attends to the wound*): If you don't keep quiet, sweetheart, I can't stitch you up . . .
FLOR DE OTOÑO: Oh, my! . . . Whatever you command, lord and master. Lead me to death and I'll follow . . .
RICARD (*To the **MEDIC***): How's it going?
MEDIC: Quite a slash . . . it's going to take more than ten stitches. I'll do the best I can in an emergency.
RICARD: You are a kind soul.
FLOR DE OTOÑO: Where are you from, you Moorish beauty?
MEDIC: Me? From Granada. But keep still so I can sew you up . . .

(*We hear a whistle through the front window. It's **SURROCA**.*)

SURROCA (*From the street.*): Ricard . . .
RICARD (*Going to the window*): Now what does he want? What is it?
SURROCA: I've got a cab waiting. Listen . . .
RICARD: What?
SURROCA: Toss me one of those . . .
RICARD: One?. . . (*Looking at the shadows of the soldiers in the background*) Are you crazy?
SURROCA: Come on . . .

RICARD (*Going to the gun rack and taking a rifle,* **HE** *slips it through the window*): Here. (**HE** *drops the rifle to* **SURROCA** *who seems to catch it in mid-air.*)
MEDIC (*Who has finished bandaging the wound*): So . . . now get him to a doctor. This will do for now.
RICARD (*Taking a bill from his wallet*): Here, friend . . .
MEDIC: No, señor . . . I can't accept it.
RICARD: Just for a coffee and brandy.
MEDIC: Shit . . . I can buy a thousand drinks with that.
RICARD: Then invite those guys. (*Referring to the soldiers.*)
MEDIC: Well, if you put it that way . . . but we're not supposed to . . . (*Takes the bill.*)
FLOR DE OTOÑO: Ooohh, I can't speak. I'm hoarse. I've lost my voice.

(**SURROCA** *enters and joins them.*)

SURROCA: The cab's waiting. (*As* **HE** *passes by the gun rack,* **HE** *snitches another rifle and puts it under his topcoat.*) Come on!
RICARD: We're deeply touched. We won't forget this. I must suggest to my friend the Captain General that he give the troop a special dinner.
MEDIC: I only did what was necessary, and I hope the young gentleman gets well soon.
SURROCA: Our respects to the lieutenant.

(*As* **HE** *passes by the gun rack again,* **HE** *grabs and hides yet another rifle. They have left the rack practically empty.*)

FLOR DE OTOÑO: Don't I get to review the troops?
SURROCA: Do you think this is *The Love Parade*? You're not Jeanette MacDonald.

(*Nevertheless, the* **SOLDIERS** *get up to bid them goodbye and line up to make a passage to the door.*)

ONE RECRUIT: Goodbye, sweetheart!
ANOTHER RECRUIT: Take care of that throat!
A THIRD RECRUIT: Don't forget to gargle . . .
FLOR DE OTOÑO (*Waving his hand*): All of you, every last one of you, will have my autographed picture . . . you darlings! Long live the Spanish army!

(***THEY*** *exit rather hurriedly. The gun rack looks totally empty. They've taken them all.*)

LIGHTS DOWN

Flor de Otoño, Teatro Español, Madrid, December 1982. Dir. Antonio Díaz Zamora. Set design by Carlos Cytrinowsky. Photo by Manuel Martínez Muñoz.

PART TWO

Another newspaper page appears with the following news items. In headlines:
NEW LIGHT ON THE ASTURIANITA CRIME. *In smaller letters: "The presumed killer of Arsenio Puig, also known as La Asturianita, is one of his own associates who hides under the alias Flor de Otoño and apparently murdered him over a supposed love rivalry, according to the testimony of a friend of the victim. The police expect to apprehend the said Flor de Otoño who has been performing at the Bataclan Cabaret. The establishment has been closed by order of the Civil Governor." Another line below in smaller letters. "We are happy to print a correction. New information on the crime permits us to rectify the unfounded suspicions that fell, perhaps intentionally, on the person of a son of a respected family, a distinguished attorney of our city. We are happy to be the first to express our regrets for such a deplorable error, imputed to malicious sources. Our most profound apology to said family, which has always enjoyed the highest esteem of our citizens." Another item:* **"Arms stolen from the Atarazanas Barracks."** *Three unscrupulous individuals assaulted the Atarazanas Military Barracks last night and carried off a variety of weapons. Through trickery, one of the malefactors, without doubt anarchist gunmen, pretended to be wounded, and while he was being treated by a medical assistant, his accomplices burglarized the gun racks of the guard post. It appears that some relationship exists between this group and the fugitive murderer of La Asturianita."*

An advertisement:"BUSTO LAXATIVE WORKS BEST FOR CONSTIPATION" Another advertisement: "PATHE PALACE: Now playing. THE LOVE PARADE, *with Maurice Chevalier and Jeanette MacDonald." Another advertisement: "LICEU OPERA HOUSE. Revival of* LA TRAVIATA. *First appearance of the renowned soprano Toti dal Monti." Another advertisement: "WAGONS LITS COOK."*

When the projections fade, the **CAÑELLAS FAMILY** *appears reunited. The same family we saw on another occasion. With the same funereal and crepuscular character. The same coffee and tea cups. The shadow of the same servant going and coming. The same operatic roulades.* **DOÑA NURIA** *is finishing a sensational reading of the newspaper item.*

DOÑA NURIA (*Triumphantly*)**:** "New information on the crime permits us to rectify the unfounded suspicions that fell, perhaps intentionally (**SHE** emphasizes this.) . . . on the person of a son of a respected (*Stressed.*) family, a distinguished attorney of our city. We are happy to be the first to express our regrets for such a deplorable error imputed to malicious sources (*Stressed.*). Our most profound apology to said family, which has always enjoyed the highest esteem of our citizens."

(*A general sigh of satisfaction. DOÑA NURIA puts the newspaper down and contemplates the others with imperious mien.*)

THE PLUMP LADY: Thanks to our blessed Lord.
THE BLOND LADY: Amen.
THE HUNCHBACKED GENTLEMAN: Gràcies a Deu.
THE FAT GENTLEMAN: Ah, yes, all's well. But . . . now we must sue for distress and damages.
THE SKINNY GENTLEMAN: Oh, we certainly must!
THE FAT GENTLEMAN: Then, with a rectification, everything would be put in order.
THE BLOND LADY (*Tearfully*): We have suffered tremendously . . .
THE FAT GENTLEMAN: Our businesses, our respected businesses, have suffered a loss to their respectability and someone should pay . . . ·
THE SKINNY GENTLEMAN: Oh, for certain!
THE PLUMP LADY: How shameful!
THE BLOND LADY: The Puigs and the Devallas snubbed me at the opera the other night.
THE FAT GENTLEMAN: It can't be permitted! Really! With a suitable compensation the problem's solved. Ja et daran!
THE HUNCHBACKED GENTLEMAN: We'll demand it, we'll demand a good indemnization. But of course. And, we must put the police on the trail of that Flor de Otoño, whom I happen to know! . . .

(*A general stir.*)

DOÑA NURIA: What are you saying? That you know that individual from the underworld?
THE HUNCHBACKED GENTLEMAN: I know that she works or used to work at a cabaret on the Paralelo . . .
THE FAT GENTLEMAN: At the Bataclan, the newspaper says so quite clearly.
THE BLOND LADY: Really? Have you ever gone to the Bataclan? Huh? Have you?
THE HUNCHBACKED GENTLEMAN: I? Mare de Deu! What are you saying?
THE BLOND LADY: Well, then, why did you say you knew her? Huh? Oh, such a man! . . .

DOÑA NURIA (*Conciliatory*): Hush, now, hush...
THE BLOND LADY (*Tearfully*): Oh, and God knows who else has gone! Have you gone with that . . . with that woman? (*SHE strikes her husband on the arm with her fists.*)
THE HUNCHBACKED GENTLEMAN: Just shut up, woman. Really!
THE BLOND LADY: This will be the death of me! . . .
THE FAT GENTLEMAN: That doesn't matter now, my dear. What we must do now is demand indemnization for distress and damages . . . Why, Lluiset himself can handle it. He's an attorney.
DOÑA NURIA: All in due course . . . in due course. Now all of you listen to me, listen. The most important thing is to regain the family's honor.
THE PLUMP LADY: Oh, indeed regain the family's honor!
DOÑA NURIA: Silence. The family's honor, the honor of Lluiset, who you may rest assured will come down hard on whoever may have been the authors of this infamy . . .
THE HUNCHBACKED GENTLEMAN: And such infamy it is!
DOÑA NURIA: So be it, the important thing will be dealt with. Now what we must do is give thanks to God, and I propose this: the entire family must go to Montserrat and give thanks to the Black Madonna . . . every member of the family!

(*A general stir.*)

THE PLUMP LADY: Oh, yes, yes. That's fine . . . to Montserrat.
THE FAT GENTLEMAN: A great idea. That first of all. We'll go to the Black Madonna and everyone can see our pain . . .
THE HUNCHBACKED GENTLEMAN: Tomorrow without fail . . .
THE BLOND LADY: Oh, you can go, but it will be alone.
DOÑA NURIA: Everyone goes. It's settled. The whole family will go to Monserrat to give thanks to the Blessed Virgin.

(***THEY*** *all stand and intone the first lines of the "Virolai"—the Catalan hymn to the Virgin of Montserrat. The "Virolai" grows louder as the lights fade on the scene.*)

DOÑA NURIA *alone.* ***SHE*** *is crying. Seated at a desk, in light filtered through the blinds of the bay windows, afternoon light,* ***SHE*** *resembles a lady painted by Rusiñol or Ramón Casas. The* ***SERVANT*** *enters. And thus begins a scene like one in a drawing-room drama by Benavente.*
PILAR: Señora, señora . . . A gentleman, who wants to see you.
DOÑA NURIA: I've told you, Pilar, that I'm receiving no one today. I refuse.
PILAR: Señora, he's probably bringing news of the young master.

DOÑA NURIA (*Stops crying*): What are you saying? Really?
PILAR: I think he's a friend of the young master. May I tell him to come in?
DOÑA NURIA: What's he like? Is he young?
PILAR: Young and quite nice.
DOÑA NURIA: Is he alone?
PILAR: Alone, yes, señora. May I tell him to come in?
DOÑA NURIA: Go, tell him to come in. (***PILAR** leaves hurriedly.* ***DOÑA NURIA*** *gets up and looks at herself in the mirror.*) I look awful!

(***PILAR'S VOICE****: "This way, sir." And **RICARD**, Lluiset's friend, enters.* ***HE*** *is dressed spiffily and bows very ceremoniously. But his large moustache and sideburns suggest a gigolo.*)

RICARD: Doña Nuria de Cañellas?
DOÑA NURIA: At your service . . .
RICARD: I've come on behalf of your son.
DOÑA NURIA: Lluiset? Oh, do sit down, please, my good man.
RICARD: I work with your son and consider him my friend. I am his law clerk.
DOÑA NURIA: Oh, a pleasure, I'm so happy to meet you . . .
RICARD: And as I imagine you must be distraught without news of your son, I got into my Rolls-Royce and here I am to bring you news . . . (***HE*** *takes a letter from his jacket pocket.*)
DOÑA NURIA: Oh, young man, you don't know how grateful I am. You have no idea what I've been going through! Has anything happened to him? Tell me . . .
RICARD: He's fine. He's perfectly fine. Do read this letter . . .
DOÑA NURIA: Oh, thank God, thank God! . . . (*Calling out.*) Pilar, Pilar!

(*The **SERVANT**, who was listening behind the door, enters overjoyed.*)

PILAR: You see, señora, you see he's all right?
DOÑA NURIA: Oh, how I've suffered! The Virgin of Monserrat has heard me . . .
PILAR: What does the letter say?
RICARD: Do read it.
DOÑA NURIA: Oh, I'm so nervous! (***SHE*** *unfolds the letter.*). "Dearest Mama" . . . (***SHE*** *breaks into tears.*)
RICARD: Do you want me to read it for you?
DOÑA NURIA: Oh, yes, thank you, young man, you are so kind. It's obvious that you're a gentleman. Pilar, bring the young man a cup of coffee. An aperitif?

Autumn Flower - 39

RICARD: Don't bother, please.
DOÑA NURIA: Bother, indeed!... But what does the letter say?
RICARD (*Reading*): "Dearest Mama"...
DOÑA NURIA (*Interrupting*): Fill meu!
RICARD: "As I imagine you're probably worried not hearing from me, I'm sending this missive with my friend and companion, Ricard, to let you know that I'm fine, that nothing has happened to me"...
DOÑA NURIA: Oh, blessed Virgin!
RICARD: "... and that I've gone to Badalona to rest a few days and to recuperate from the unpleasantness those wicked people caused me. I'm with some good friends, the bearer of this letter who is, as you will see, a stupendous fellow, and some others. Don't worry and just let me have some quiet for a few days. I need some rest after all that's happened. I love you very, very much, and I send you lots of kisses. Your son, Lluiset."
DOÑA NURIA: Oh, poor boy. He's so good.
PILAR: Oh, how happy I am, ma'am!... (*To RICARD*) Now I'll bring your coffee.
RICARD (*Handing the letter to DOÑA NURIA*): Don't bother. If I didn't come before, it was because I couldn't.
DOÑA NURIA: So they're at the country house? I don't know if they'll have enough covers for the beds and...
RICARD: Don't worry, señora, everything's fine.
DOÑA NURIA: I think I should go lend a hand...
RICARD: No, no, dear lady, please. We love living the Bohemian life, and it's all quite divine.
DOÑA NURIA (*Laughing*): Oh, you young people! You young people! Well, yes, I was worried not knowing where that child of mine had gone. Yesterday we were at Montserrat, and I would have so liked to have him beside me.
RICARD: We wanted to let you know yesterday, but with the distance...
DOÑA NURIA: Well, the fact is he's all right.
RICARD: It's a matter of only a few days, to rest...
DOÑA NURIA: He does need rest, poor boy, with what he's endured. Have you seen how bad people can be?
RICARD: One must forget all that.
DOÑA NURIA (*With a sweep of her lorgnette*): And you, young man, have you known my Lluiset for long?
RICARD: Oh, since our university days. We've worked together in attorney Peracamps's law office.
DOÑA NURIA: Oh! Then you must know my son quite well. He is so good, so innocent.
RICARD: Oh, indeed, señora! A priceless companion.

DOÑA NURIA: It's not just because I'm his mother, but everyone must say the same things about him. Good, intelligent, polite, one of a kind . . . well, present company excepted.
RICARD: Please, señora.
DOÑA NURIA: I can see that you yourself have nothing to envy in him. I well know that my son doesn't associate with just anyone.
RICARD: Oh, no, señora. That's true. Your son is too serious . . .
DOÑA NURIA: Oh, indeed! You can say that again. Too serious, too serious, I'd say. Don't you agree? A boy so young, and so independent, who leads the life of a monk, a monk. That's what worries me a bit.

(*The SERVANT enters with a tray and a cup of coffee.*)

DOÑA NURIA (*To the SERVANT*)**:** Why haven't you used the silver tray?
PILAR: Oh, señora, I'm so overcome with happiness that I . . .
RICARD: Dear lady, please.
DOÑA NURIA: Well, as I was saying, young man, that is what bothers me about the boy, that he doesn't have fun, that he's not like the others who have their times for relaxation, who enjoy themselves. He's so studious, always in his bachelor's apartment, at his work . . . Oh, I don't know, I'd like for him to have a bit of amusement. Except for the opera, he . . .
RICARD: Oh, don't worry, señora, there'll be time for that.
DOÑA NURIA: But he's already thirty . . .
RICARD: What we must do now is make a future for ourselves, and afterwards . . .
DOÑA NURIA: Oh, yes! A future. Yes, indeed. I can see that you're very sensible. It's obvious my Lluiset knows how to choose his friends. (*RICARD nods his head in agreement.*) But I'd like for both of you to have a little amusement. To waste something other than money . . . What about romances? Because that's a subject my Lluiset never mentions.
RICARD (*Archly*)**:** Oh, take no notice of that, those are carried on in secret.
DOÑA NURIA: Is there some young lady in the picture now?
RICARD (*Very mischievously*)**:** Those are very intimate matters and . . .
DOÑA NURIA: Oh, but nothing should be hidden from a mother. So you do have some gay adventures? Oh, you rascals, you rascals . . . Well, he's going to hear a word or two from me for not telling me about all this.
RICARD: Well, it's just a lot of silly things, you know . . .
DOÑA NURIA (*Very happy*)**:** Yes, silly things. But it would be terrible if some minx took advantage of him. And since he's so kindhearted. As long as it's not some chorus girl, or something like that.
RICARD: Please, señora, we don't frequent places like that.

Autumn Flower - 41

DOÑA NURIA: I'm so glad, I'm so glad you're enjoying yourselves without going too far. You don't know what a pleasure it's been to meet you. You don't know. You must drop by more often . . .
RICARD: I'm always so busy . . .
DOÑA NURIA: Ah, that's fine! But occasionally one should go out for a little fling.
RICARD: I do when I can . . .
DOÑA NURIA: You're a bit timid, like Lluiset.
RICARD: Well, not exactly timid . . .
DOÑA NURIA: Yes, yes, you can't fool me, for I've seen a lot in my time. You're timid and good. The right companion for my Lluiset, but you must keep each other's spirits up.
RICARD: Oh, we do that, to be sure . . .
DOÑA NURIA: And tell me, aren't you Catalan?
RICARD: Yes, señora, I was born in Vilanova, my parents . . .
DOÑA NURIA: Then why don't you speak Catalan?
RICARD: Oh, I don't know, since it's not spoken at the office, I'm just not used to it.
DOÑA NURIA: Oh, of course. Like my Lluiset . . . Oh, you don't know, you don't know what a joy it's been for you to bring me news and also, of course, to meet a young man with such fine qualities as yours!
RICARD: Señora, señora! . . . (*The light fades to darkness.*)

The Poble Nou Workers' Cooperative. Salon of a bar with great neogothic windows that look out on the working-class neighborhood. Marble tables where the workers sit to have their coffee and brandy and a game of cards between shifts at the factory. Anarchist signs and political posters on the walls. ("Property is Theft", etc.) Sindacalist acronyms and the escutcheon of the "Clavé Chorale." A gramophone horn opens up like an exotic flower. Popular sumptuousness that has seen better days. Dense smoke. Grim faces of political hotheads. Restless shadows around a billiard table. Behind the counter of spotless marble, like a flower in the mud, a robust **LASS** *is blossoming at sixteen as a hope for peace and happiness in the sinister ambience of an anarchist, industrial neighborhood. Next to one of the windows* **FLOR DE OTOÑO-LLUISET** *is sitting, dressed in a hybrid get-up, part street smart and part gangster garb: an elegant cap, a scarf knotted coquettishly around his neck, and a checked, close-fitting sweater that outlines his pectorals and waist. Gray pants, white shoes. If he weren't in such a place, he could be a sportsman from Monte Carlo.* **SURROCA** *is amusing himself with a battery radio that extends its wires over his big head and covers his ears with enormous earphones.* **RICARD**, *with a flowing top coat over his shoulders, his soft-*

brimmed Bohemian hat pushed back gangster style, is giving the news of the day.)

RICARD: You can rest easy.
LLUISET: A mother is a mother. (*HE hums "Nen de la Mare" or "Mother's Child."*)
RICARD: Your mother's very nice. It broke my heart to hear her talk . . .
LLUISET: Poor dear! . . .
RICARD: All that business about family is so old-fashioned.
LLUISET: What do you expect? I'm an anarchist, an anarchist. But she has a good heart.
SURROCA (*Shouting excitedly*): I've got it . . . I've got it!
LLUISET (*Jumping*): Really! You frightened me!
SURROCA: You can hear it . . . you can hear it!
LLUISET: He's been like that all morning. What a pain.

(*Four grim, sinister-looking MEN have arrived. Grimy felt hats, loose shirts, belts girding their loins. The GIRL from the bar leads them like a common man's Beatrice toward the camouflaged men.*)

GIRL: Senyor Ricard, these gentlemen are asking for you.
RICARD (*Getting up*): Oh, yes. Sit down, fellows, have a seat. (*To LLUISET.*) Well, we've got them here.

(*The FOUR MEN remain standing, either from respect or because THEY prefer not to mix with a certain kind of people.*)

CATALAN PORTER (*A fat man with a Catalan-type cap*): Senyó Ricard, I bring you the cream of the Born Market and the neighborhood. (*HE shows the "merchandise," which are the other three. THEY say hello with a kind of grunt.*)
GIRL (*Who has remained at a distance*): Would the gentlemen like anything? Coffee with brandy?
CATALAN PORTER: We'll order something in a minute, in a minute . . .

(*The other MEN look at the young GIRL, and we see their hands reach out toward her buttocks as SHE walks seductively back to the bar.*)

RICARD: Since you don't want to sit down . . .
CATALAN PORTER: There's still a lot of work to do.
GALICIAN PORTER: We're ready to hear what you gents want . . .
RICARD (*To LLUISET*): You tell them . . . He's the boss here.

(*LLUISET has been observing the solid build of the four porters and adjusting the scarf around his neck.*)

CATALAN PORTER (*With a slight nod*): Glad to meet yuh, senyó.

(*Grunts from the other MEN.*)

LLUISET (*With a little wink*): They seem perfect for the job. You explain, Ricard, and you all must excuse me. I have a headache . . .
RICARD: Well, then . . . Sebastian has probably told you something . . .
CATALAN PORTER: Yeah, senyó. But if yuh don't mind, speak real clear because these guys are from all over and they won't understand half you say. Right?

(*Grunts from the Andalusian-Galician-Murcian **TRIO** who really are half out of it.*)

RICARD: Fine, I'll repeat everything if I have to, so it'll be clear to them. It's all about administering a corrective to a certain individual, in everyday language, beat up the guy.
CATALAN PORTER: What we call "roughing up."
ANDALUSIAN PORTER: Take the starch outta 'em.
GALICIAN PORTER: A good lickin'.
MURCIAN PORTER (*Self-satisfied and effusive*): All that stuff and beat him to a pulp . . . yeah! Yeah!
CATALAN PORTER: Well, senyó, we get the idea, so give us the details and the deal's done.
RICARD (*Taking a photo from his back pant's pocket*): This is the guy. Any chance you know him?
CATALAN PORTER (*Taking out some eyeglasses and putting them on, **HE** looks at the photo solemnly.*): At the moment . . .

(*The **TRIAD** of heads leans over to see the photo.*)

RICARD: He's the one who ran around with La Asturianita, the one from the Barrio Chino.
ANDALUSIAN PORTER (*With a regional lisp*): Yeah, señó, sure. I worked for the guy. Sure, yours truly was his organ grinder when this son of bitch was in the music business.
CATALAN PORTER: It's all the same. Just tell us who he is, when and where he'll be . . . and that does it.

RICARD: He frequents the cabarets on the Paralelo.

CATALAN PORTER: Don't you worry, we'll get him. Soon as . . .

LLUISET (*Putting in a word very nervously*): A good beating. A fantastic one he won't forget, one hell of a beating . . .

CATALAN PORTER: You don't have to tell me anything, senyoreto, I'll take care of everything. It'll be a toss up whether he goes to the hospital or the cemetery.

LLUISET (*Pressing his temples*): Oh, friend, don't mention that word in my presence, cemetery . . .

(***SURROCA*** *has a wild look as he listens through the earphones, and the* ***PORTERS*** *watch him stupefied.*)

RICARD (*Moving with the* ***WORKERS*** *to the bar*): You get the point. Rough him up, take him down a peg or two, so he won't be cocky anytime soon.

CATALAN PORTER: You bet, senyó, you bet. I know the type. I think you gentlemen will get satisfaction . . .

RICARD: But no scandal, no complications.

CATALAN PORTER: No way.

RICARD: As for the money . . .

CATALAN PORTER (*Catching his drift*): About that . . . Look, I'll give it to you straight. Us fellows make our living in the Born, we're porters, for sure, because we don't know how to do anything else. But if we're going to lose a day's pay . . .

RICARD: Sure, sure, you'll get that day's pay and more . . .

CATALAN PORTER: Then it's settled. The rest is up to you.

GALICIAN PORTER: Where I come from we don't mess with anybody for less than five pesos.

RICARD (*Trying to draw them all into an embrace*): Don't worry, you're all going to be satisfied. Tell us the amount of a day's wages, which we'll compensate along with half the payment now . . . and the other half when the job's done.

CATALAN PORTER: Let's not argue, for shit, we're all friends here.

RICARD: All friends, and we're talking about an enemy of the people, as that one said, a bloodsucker of the workers. (*Pointing to the* ***ANDALUSIAN***.)

ANDALUSIAN PORTER (*Interrupting*): The fucking bastard, I'll slit his face open or my name's not Manolo.

CATALAN PORTER: Yeah, senyó. A bourgeois bastard. It's all the same if we send him to the other world, if you don't mind me saying so.

RICARD: Bravo! Now for drinks. Nena, treat these gentlemen.

GIRL: What do you want?

ANDALUSIAN PORTER: Brandy for me, cutie.

(*The voices fade as the **MEN** become involved in their free drinks, and **RICARD** returns to his two friends. Meanwhile, **SURROCA** has handed the earphones to **LLUISET**, who makes a face.*)

SURROCA: It sounds great, maca! (*Putting the earphones on **LLUISET**.*) Here. Some tango!
LLUISET: Oh, leave me alone! What a nuisance! I can't hear a thing, nothing . . .
SURROCA (*Infuriated*)**:** So! Give them back.
LLUISET: Wait . . . (*With a little cry*) Oh, yes, I can hear! . . . A tango . . . (*Sings along*) "Yo soy la morocha—la más apreciada—la más agraciada de la población . . ."
RICARD (*Punching him lightly on the shoulder*)**:** Listen, you. This . . .
LLUISET (*Brushing him away with a flip of his hand, **HE** goes on singing.*)**:** "Soy la morocha argentina . . ."
SURROCA: That's enough, you've heard it, now give them back.
LLUISET (*Taking off the earphones and handing them to him*)**:** Here, take them . . . What a song bird! Really, now!
RICARD (*To **LLUISET***)**:** I said they've got their instructions. They're going to give the guy a bellyache.
LLUISET (*With sadistic pleasure*)**:** Oh, poor thing!
RICARD (*Looking through the front windows*)**:** And the others are here now. (*To **SURROCA**.*) Hey, you, leave off that now, we're going to get things underway.

(*Three other characters enter. They are young, madcap **STUDENTS**. Dissipated, with dark circles under their eyes, they are wearing gangster-style hats pushed back on their heads.*)

FIRST STUDENT (Giving **RICARD** *a pat on the back*)**:** Oh, man! What a trip!
RICARD: Greetings, friends. Sit down. What have you got there?
SECOND STUDENT (*Who is carrying a round object wrapped in a newspaper*)**:** A ball, to play a little game with.
THIRD STUDENT (*Who is blond and looks as if **HE** just arrived from Oxford*)**:** The guy's built a bomb.
LLUISET: A bomb? Ay, mi madre!
FIRST STUDENT: It's a winter watermelon. Toss it over here.

(*The **SECOND STUDENT** throws the package, and the **FIRST STUDENT** catches it gracefully.*)

RICARD: Don't fuck around. Is it real? What is it?
THIRD STUDENT: A bomb. We already told you. To start the festivities. As soon as it explodes . . .
SECOND STUDENT: I have an uncle who makes fireworks in Valencia.
RICARD: Cut the joking, clown. The question is . . .

(*SURROCA has put aside his radio and is beginning to get interested in the conversation.*)

FIRST STUDENT: We're ready. It's all fixed.
RICARD (*To LLUISET*): What do you say?
LLUISET (*Putting his hand to his head*): Whew! I've got a headache. (*Suddenly becoming serious.*) What about the factory?
FIRST STUDENT (*Smacking his lips*): Everything's ready. Light the fuse and it'll burn like a bonfire.
LLUISET (*Rubbing his hands together enthusiastically*): My poor hunchbacked uncle. And what about the workers?
FIRST STUDENT: They'll strike. Every group . . . all of them go on strike, as soon as the fuse is lit.
SECOND STUDENT: The School of Law and the School of Medicine are joining the strike.
THIRD STUDENT: The anarchist unions are making common cause with us to oppose capitalism and the inquisition.
FIRST STUDENT (*Tapping the SECOND STUDENT on the shoulder*): Throw it here, chum.
SECOND STUDENT (*Tossing the wrapped object to him*): For the goal . . .
FIRST STUDENT (*Catching the object*): As soon as this bargain explodes (*Pointing to the wrapped object.*) all of Poble Nou will go up in flames. Give the land back to the people!

(*The bar is filled with dim, lurking silhouettes. A feeling of great events about to take place is hanging in the air.*)

SURROCA (*Looking longingly at his radio*): Just when the sound was getting clearer.
LLUISET: You're so capricious. The anarchist revolution is about to triumph and all you can think about is your radio.
RICARD: And what about Vilanova?
FIRST STUDENT: Terrific! The Club there will derail the express train from Madrid, the Sudexprés.

LLUISET (*With a little cry*): How scary! And the Serracant Perfumes factory, what time will it happen?
FIRST STUDENT: You see this? (*Showing the wrapped object.*) When this explodes, fire.
LLUISET: Oh, then, I ought to let my uncle the hunchback know!
RICARD: Don't make me laugh.
SECOND STUDENT: Well, who's inviting us for a drink? We're not going to the trenches without fortifying ourselves a little.
RICARD: Nena, bring three brandies.
SURROCA (*Excited*): The bourgeoisie don't know what's in store for them.
RICARD (*To the STUDENTS*): We've distributed arms from the Atarazanas Barracks.
FIRST STUDENT (*Laughing with delight*): From Atarazanas? You guys really have balls.
SECOND STUDENT (*Playing with the wrapped object and singing*): "I'll light it for you, you cheeky guy, I've got the fire right here . . . " (*HE stops in midsong because two CIVIL GUARDS suddenly enter, leaving the personnel of the cooperative dumbstruck.*)

(*A silence comes over the bar. The STUDENT with the object stands like a Greek statue holding a ball in his hands, because the GUARDS are coming straight to them.*)

FIRST GUARD: What's going on here?

(*The silence thickens. The GIRL at the bar has also become frozen with a cup in her hand.*)

LLUISET (*Who is the first to recover*): Going on? Nothing's going on, officer . . . Would you like a drink?
FIRST GUARD (*To the STUDENTS*): You, show me some identification.
FIRST STUDENT: Us?
SECOND GUARD (*More conciliatory*): Didn't you hear what he said?
RICARD (*With a big smile*): These are some friends of mine, from Vilanova.
FIRST GUARD: I'm not interested in where they came from.
LLUISET: Oh, my goodness!
SECOND GUARD (*To LLUISET*): You just keep your mouth shut for a minute.
FIRST GUARD: Come on, your papers.
SECOND STUDENT (*Offering the package to the FIRST STUDENT*): Take this, I can't unbutton my jacket.
FIRST STUDENT (*Pretending fright*): Don't give that thing to me . . .

FIRST GUARD (*Striking the table with his fist*): Cut the smart talk!
SECOND STUDENT (*Tossing the package to **LLUISET***): Here, you take it.
LLUISET (*With a cry*): Oh, my God, the bomb!
FIRST GUARD (*Now angry*): Cut out the funny stuff! (*Pointing to the package.*) What the hell is that?
LLUISET: A bomb, officer, a bomb.
SECOND GUARD (*Conciliatory*): Now, fellow, that's not something to be joking about.
SURROCA: He's always trying to be funny.
FIRST GUARD: You can all come with us to headquarters.
FIRST STUDENT: Whatever you say, sergeant. Bring the bomb . . .
SECOND STUDENT: Leave the bomb here.
LLUISET: We'll take the bomb.
FIRST GUARD (*Taking the package from **LLUISET***): No more horsing around. The fun's over. You know who gives orders here. Everyone outside. Better unholster your pistol, Felipe.

(*While the **SECOND GUARD** reluctantly takes out his pistol, the **CONSPIRATORS** stand up.*)

LLUISET: We'll go wherever you wish. But don't say we didn't warn you, don't say we didn't, because what you've got in those delicate hands is a bomb, a real bomb.
FIRST GUARD: The shit you say! I'll get rid of the thing. (***HE** throws the bomb through the front window into the street, and a second later there is a horrendous explosion, shattering the windows, knocking over tables, sending the characters reeling and plunging the scene into darkness.*)

(*Shots in the darkness, shouts from the anarchists, hymns, the hoofbeats of horses, the ringing of the firetruck, drunken voices, etc. In the midst of the pandemonium, the lights come on again on the scene and the cooperative has been turned into a war zone. Broken glass. Tables turned into a barricade. The molding is bullet scared; even the anarchist posters have suffered the effects of the revolution, and the slogan "Property is Theft" now reads "Prop is Theft." **LLUISET, SURROCA, RICARD,** the **STUDENTS,** the **PORTERS,** and other dim individuals fight like jungle beasts, aiming their rifles through the windows and from behind the improvised barricades. The bar **GIRL** stands white and fragile amidst the broken glass of the counter, scared to death and emitting sobs that serve as counterpoint to the gunshots, blasphemies, and oaths of the combattants. The spraddled legs of one of the **CIVIL GUARDS,** killed in the first assault, stick out from under a broken sofa. Dense gunpowder smoke and heroism hang over it all.*)

LLUISET (*Firing a small lady's pistol*): They won't take us, they won't!
RICARD: Hurray for liberal Communism!
LLUISET (*Rising up very heroically*): Here we are, here we are!
SURROCA: You've messed up my radio, but I got a few of you.
PORTER RIFLEMAN: Death to the bloodsucking bourgeosie!
ANOTHER RIFLEMAN: Hurray for free Catalonia!
ANOTHER RIFLEMAN: We'll beat the shit out of you!
SURROCA: Take that, kiddo.
A STUDENT: Lackeys of the bourgeoisie!
ANOTHER STUDENT: Authority is shittt!
GIRL: Ai, mare meva! Mare meva! Oh, blessed Virgin!
LLUISET (*Turning around*): Keep quiet, nena, keep quiet!
A PORTER RIFLEMAN (*In the spirit of fabled Numancia*): The blood of martyrs will bring us a libertarian springtime!
SEVERAL RIFLEMEN: Hurray for a comrade like you!
SURROCA (*To LLUISET*): Get that one, he's closest to you. The one with the pompom, aim, fire . . .
LLUISET (*Closing his eyes*): I hit him . . .
CHORUS OF RIFLEMEN: The poor of the world rise up!

(*Horrendous cacaphony.*)

VOICES FROM OUTSIDE: Brothers, we'll liberate you, we'll set you free!
LLUISET: Don't listen to them, comrades, they're sirens to lure us.
SEVERAL RIFLEMEN: Sons of bitches, sons of bitches, sons of bitches!
PORTER RIFLEMAN (*Going berserk*): We'll show the sons of bitches!
GIRL (*Screaming in fear*): Ai, mare meva! I want to get out of here!
LLUISET: Shut up, dear, and bring me a glass of water. I'm parched.
GIRL: Oh, senyoreto . . .
LLUISET: Forget the "senyoreto" and bring me some water.
RICARD: Get it yourself. Can't you see the girl's scared out of her wits?
LLUISET: The rest of you hold the fort, I'm going to the rearguard . . . (*HE retreats to the bar, pushes the GIRL aside and pours a glass of water.*) You're really scared, aren't you, nena?
GIRL (*Throwing her arms around him*): Oh, senyor, I want to go home.
LLUISET (*Offering her water*): It's going to be all right, nena, it will. Here, have a sip.
SURROCA (*Firing feverishly*): What an attack!
RICARD: Free men onward!
A STUDENT: And where are the poets? Where are the poets who sing of freedom?

ANOTHER STUDENT: The poets? They're under the bed.
A PORTER RIFLEMAN: Damn it to hell! It's jammed on me again. These rifles from the barracks aren't worth shit!
ANOTHER VOLUNTEER: Pull back on the bolt.
THE PORTER RIFLEMAN: I did already, fuck it!
THE OTHER ONE: Bring it here . . . (*At that moment the rifle explodes and wounds both of them.*)
ANDALUSIAN PORTER: Fuck it all, we've lost two, but there're some of us left who're worth five of those bastards!
A STUDENT: You said it, chum.
A RIFLEMAN: For libertarian Communism!
AN IMPROVISED CHORUS: Hurray for bread, hurray for wine, and hurray for us all!
LLUISET (*Who has his arms around the **GIRL**, soothing her*): Don't be afraid, nena. Don't you see that we're fighting for you and all the girls like you? We're fighting so there'll be no more bloodshed, no more rapes, no more hunger, no more . . .
GIRL (*Bent over and looking up at **LLUISET***): I'm still afraid . . .
LLUISET (*Patting her*): You'll see, when you're grown up, you'll be happier and you can live in peace with the man you want, with your children. . . Can't you see, nena, that we're fighting so that everybody can be happy?
GIRL (*Beginning to be consoled*): Yes, now I do, yes . . .
LLUISET: Doncs, noia . . . So there.
A RIFLEMAN: These shitty military rifles!
RICARD: Maybe they are, but don't look a gift horse in the mouth.
A PORTER RIFLEMAN (*His face covered with blood, **HE** begins to leap over the debris*): The sons of bitches got me, the sons of bitches got me.
ANOTHER PORTER: Get down, fellow.
THE WOUNDED MAN (*Starting to throw pieces of marble from the broken tables through the window*): Murderers! You think you've got us cornered.
FIRST STUDENT: Courage, comrade, your blood is the blood of a new freedom!.
AN ECHO: A new freedom! . . .
LLUISET (*To the **GIRL***): A new freedom. That's what we'll make, you'll see, nena, you'll see how a free springtime will come and everything will be a kind of rose without thorns . . .
RICARD: Come here, you, and leave off the melodrama. Things are getting ugly.
SURROCA (*Leaping like a monkey*): You can say that again. It's really getting ugly!
A STUDENT: You'll walk over our dead bodies, that's what!

AN EXCITED RIFLEMAN: They won't win, they shall not pass, we won't let them!
LLUISET (*Trying to get away from the GIRL*): Let me go, sweet. I have to fight.
GIRL: Don't leave me, don't leave me!
LLUISET: Nena, nena . . .
AN IMPROVISED CHORUS: We've got them where we want them, we've got them . . .
ANOTHER CHORUS: Hurray for bread, hurray for wine, hurray for us all!

(*An enormous roar. Everything shakes.*)

SURROCA (*Crying out*): Artillery! The bastards have brought in artillery.

(*There is a great bustle of heroism. **LLUISET** has thrown himself on the floor with the **GIRL**. Clouds of smoke.*)

VOICES: They won't win, they shall not pass!
OTHER VOICES: They'll have to pass over our dead bodies!
OTHERS: Hold the fort, comrades! Long live libertarian Communism!

(*Artillery bursts The ground shakess. A piece of the roof collapses and the voices grow hoarser and more excited.*)

VOICES IN THE SMOKE (*Hoarse and invincible*): Hurray for bread, hurray for wine, hurray for us all! (*Thunderous din and BLACKOUT.*)

*Seated in the dock, lighted by strong spots, the three leaders of the aborted revolutionary coup of the Poble Nou, **LLUISET-FLOR DE OTOÑO, RICARD**, and **SURROCA**. We may guess that there are shadows of Civil Guard tricornes, reflections of military sabres, the sinister gloom of a military castle, and the atmosphere of a summary trial. **THEY** face forward, with the gleam of madness in their eyes that belongs to the condemned who have no hope of reprieve. Around them the sounds of voices which sometimes are broken off in midsentence; others become unintelligible; some acquire a parliamentary tone. Legal voices, journalists, the curious, whom **THEY** listen to like some doleful music unworthy of consideration.*

DRY MILITARY VOICE: Murderers, armed robbers, immoral cocaine addicts, gunmen in the hire of international crime . . .
VOICE OF A JOURNALIST: Barcelona, peaceful and progressive city of the Mediterranean, emblem of work and civic pride, adds today a sinister note to

the enlightened presence of the international tournaments: the criminal attack that some common delinquents, called anarchists, carried out to satisfy their criminal instincts and sow horror in the peaceful citizens of our industrious and fair city.

DRY MILITARY VOICE: Cocaine addicts, homosexuals, thieves, international underworld, Freemasonry, Communism . . .

VOICE OF A JOURNALIST: This land of poets and artists, this land of business men, of specific lineage, cradle of the brave, cannot shelter in its breast a lowly faction of . . .

DRY MILITARY VOICE: Separatists, members of international crime, libertarians of vice . . .

VOICE OF A JOURNALIST: Our freedoms cannot be disrupted by the proliferation of such vipers originating in the underworld of other countries, who poison our fair cities and the air of our blessed law and order . . .

DRY MILITARY VOICE: Vicious homosexuals, addicts, human outcasts who no longer deserve to be called human . . .

VOICE OF A JOURNALIST: And however painful it may be for us, the presence among the criminals of the son of an honorable family belonging to industrial society, by his own choice, blinded by the chains of vice, must not cause our desire for implacable justice to waver. We must be inflexible and remember this: "lex dura sed lex," A harsh law but it is the law.

DRY MILITARY VOICE: We shall dynamite that nefarious Barrio Chino, we'll excise the social gangrene with a single stroke.

(Now we hear people's voices, indistinct and jumbled: "Shoot them all!" "Preserve law and order!" "Tranquilitat i bons aliments . . ." "Quin horror, quin horror!" "Depraved people with no principles." "Poor Catalonia, a day of mourning for us.")

VOICE OF A CATALAN JOURNALIST: Above all, above all, our Catalonia has been affected by the accursed disorder of an insignificant group that call themselves "anarchists," and it is obvious that they are only common delinquents, murderers, and perverts, who want to take our Catalonia—now so smiling and splenderous—to the abyss of tragic violence and bloodshed.

DRY MILITARY VOICE: Death, death, death, death!

VOICE OF A CLERICAL JOURNALIST: Brothers, it is perhaps difficult with this delirium to look with compassion where there is only filth, depravity, Satanism . . . Let us ask that God's justice do what the justice of men cannot do, let us intone a hymn of penitence and say with me: miserere nobis, miserere nobis, miserere nobis . . .

DRY MILITARY VOICE (*In a decreasing whisper*): Death, death, death, death! . . .

(*The **THREE RAGAMUFFINS** in the dock, indifferent, continue defying the audience with their crazed look. Lights down.*)

A murky room in the Montjuïc Castle set up as a chapel. Hours before dawn. A sullen figure of Christ on a table with two sinister candlesticks providing light. Three makeshift beds. A table with two bottles and the remains of a meal. The shapes of the three condemned men can be made out in the faint light. **LLUISET** *is stretched out on a bed rather like an odalisque, with a scarf around his neck;* **RICARD** *straddles a chair and is immersed in his thoughts;* **SURROCA**, *with a feverish look, continues to listen to his radio, the earphones on his head. In the silence, the footsteps of a* **PRIEST** *stand out as* **HE** *measures the scene from one end to the other, occasionally stopping before the crucifix and folding his hands. A* **LIEUTENANT**, *the counsel for the defense no doubt, looks out the barred window, sabre in hand, toward the sea. There is the sound of ship horns in the harbor and the flapping of seagulls. A* **GUARD**, *a sad recruit with an army haircut, leans on his rifle and nods sleepily.*

PRIEST (*After one of his strolls, stopping in front of the condemned men*): Brothers, my brothers, have faith in God, for he is watching you . . . (*Silence.*) Just a single instant, one instant, and you will be safe. Once Jesus saw a Centurion approaching him with a sick slave . . . Listen to me, my son . (**HE** *has sat down on the edge of Lluiset's bed, startling him.*)
LLUISET: Really! What a nuisance this man is, what a night he's making us spend. Go away.

(*The **PRIEST** gets up and steps back a bit.* **HE** *remains doubtful and observes the other prisoners, not daring, because of their attitude, to attempt the salvation of their souls. The* **PRIEST**, *moving his arms, goes toward the* **LIEUTENANT**, *who gives him a friendly pat on the shoulder. The* **PRIEST** *seems to feel through the touch an Augustinian energy that brings him to kneel before the reprobates and continue his sermon.*)

PRIEST: Brothers, remember that Centurion whose slave was sick, sick and beyond hope, his slave as much a slave as we miserable beings ourselves are slaves . . . A slave he adored and loved like his own son . . .
LLUISET (*Sitting up a bit*): They loved each other?
PRIEST: They beheld each other through the goodness of God.
LLUISET: Fine. Then what?

PRIEST: Well, then, my son, the Centurion saw Jesus coming up to him and he said to him: "Lord, I have a sick slave, but I know that only you can cure him. Come, then, to my house and say a word, a single word, and my slave will be made well."
LLUISET: Hah! What brazenness . . . and without offering to pay him a thing.
PRIEST (*Not noticing*): I am showing you faith, faith in the compassion of the Lord. Just as your souls, however much they've sinned, can be healed by saying a single word . . . (*HE stands up and goes like a catapult toward LLUISET, lifting the edge of his vestment.*)
LLUISET (*Leaping from the bed and running toward the LIEUTENANT on the other side of the room*): Ai, mare meva, he's gone berserk!
PRIEST: My son, a single word!
LLUISET (*Getting closer to the LIEUTENANT and almost hugging him*): Guard, defend me!
LIEUTENANT (*Stepping back austerely in confusion*): Come now, fellow, let's see if . . .
RICARD (*Confronting the PRIEST*): Goddamn it, will you stop, man? Can't you see he's . . . ?
SURROCA (*Taking off his earphones*): They won't even let me hear the sound of the sea in the final moments of my shitty life.
PRIEST (*Who has retreated to a corner, kneeling*): Here I remain on my knees until your souls belong to the Lord. (*To the GUARD*) Give me your bayonet, son, to put under my knees for self-mortification . . .
GUARD (*Totally awake now and with a wild look as HE struggles with the PRIEST who is trying to wrest the bayonet from him*): Padre, padre, I can't . . . the rules. Lieutenant, look what he's doing! They'll shoot me!
LIEUTENANT (*Going toward the PRIEST*): Father, millitary rules forbid a soldier handing over any of his arms.
PRIEST (*Whining, still on his knees*): I want their souls, their souls ·. .

(*Gloomy silence. LLUISET stands looking through the barred window. The others remain in their same positions.*)

LLUISET: Damn, it's cold.
RICARD (*In a hoarse voice*): There's some brandy in that bottle.
LLUISET: I don't care for brandy.
RICARD: Then bring it to me.

(*LLUISET reaches for the bottle and takes it to RICARD, who drinks eagerly.*)

LLUISET: Do you love me as much as that Roman guy loved his slave?

(**RICARD** *doesn't answer. A spark of sunrise filters in. There is a chill everywhere. We hear the mutterings of the priest.* **LLUISET** *walks toward the door. The* **PRIEST** *grabs him by the wrist.*)

LLUISET (*With a little cry*): Not again!
PRIEST: You can put your hope in God, in God, you who come from a good family.
LLUISET (*Pulling free*): Damn, this guy never stops singing . . . (*Looking hard at the* **PRIEST**.) If God exists, I'll tell him you said so, dear. (**HE** *gives him an affectionate poke in the belly.*)
PRIEST (*Radiant*): Hallelujah, hallelujah, blessed, blessed!

(*The sound of keys. The doors open. The* **COMMANDANT** *enters. Sounds of military footsteps. The* **PRIEST** *and the* **LIEUTENANT** *come to attention. Clicking of heels.*)

COMMANDANT: It's time . . .

(*General sense of helplessness in which the sound of soldiers' feet in the passageway and the muted commands of a sergeant make the skin tingle. A violet light in the barred window.* **RICARD** *stands up regally.* **SURROCA** *removes his earphones and throws them scornfully on the table.*)

LIEUTENANT (*Going up to the* **COMMANDANT**): There was no reprieve?
COMMANDANT: No, there wasn't. So . . .
PRIEST (*Clasping his hands and muttering*): Sanctus, sanctus, sanctus!
COMMANDANT (*Turning to the three*): According to the rules, you may have a last wish.
RICARD (*Bellowing*): May libertarian Communism long endure!

(**SURROCA** *spits.*)

LLUISET: I . . . I . . . I want you to let me put on my lipstick.

(**THEY** *are all appalled at such a blasphemy and look at the floor.*)

PRIEST (*His words are underscored after* **LLUISET'S** *astonishing request*): Sanctus, sanctus, sanctus, sanctus . . .

(*At this point someone has called to the* **PRIEST**. **HE** *exits and then returns at the moment the* **COMMANDANT** *is about to order them to be led away.*)

*The **PRIEST** takes the **COMMANDANT** aside and whispers something in his ear. The **COMMANDANT** shakes his head in surprise and looks at his wrist-watch.*)

COMMANDANT: Five minutes, but only five minutes . . .

(*The **PRIEST** exits again with long strides.*)

COMMANDANT: Don Luis de Serracant . . .
LLUISET (*With a certain brazenness*)**:** That's my name.
COMMANDANT: You are to receive a farewell visit.
LLUISET: I? . . .
COMMNDANT: You have five minutes. (*To the **LIEUTENANT**.*) Take the others out.

(*The **LIEUTENANT** goes toward **RICARD** and **SURROCA**, gesturing to them that they are to leave. At the moment **THEY** are exiting, **DOÑA NURIA CAÑELLAS** enters, dressed elegantly in purple velvet, with a hat and a little veil. Without taking notice of anything else, **SHE** rushes to her son. **LLUISET**, after a moment of doubt, embraces his mother. The others have now left, including the **PRIEST**, and only a **CORPORAL** remains in a far corner.*)

DOÑA NURIA: Son! Fill meu! Fill meu!
LLUISET: Mare . . . Mare.
DOÑA NURIA: Why didn't you tell me you were leaving for Mexico? Thankfully, I learned by chance. If I hadn't, how could I have said goodbye to you?
LLUISET (*His willpower weakening*)**:** We're leaving for Mexico . . .
DOÑA NURIA: I had to rush to get here, son. (*Showing him a small travel bag **SHE** has in her hand.*) And since you are so absentminded, I brought you a few things: those silk pijamas, the orange ones you like so much . . .
LLUISET: How wonderful! You think of everything, Mamá.
DOÑA NURIA: And how are you going to leave dressed that way in this chilly weather? And the cool night air at sea?
LLUISET (*Going along with the act*)**:** It's not really so cold.
DOÑA NURIA: It's cold on ships . . . Please take care of yourself, son.
LLUISET: Don't worry, don't worry. I will.
DOÑA NURIA: There's also some cologne inside, some perfume . . . and lipstick.
LLUISET: Mamá, you never miss a thing.

DOÑA NURIA: Because on the ship, you must see other people. How long is the crossing?
LLUISET: A month.
DOÑA NURIA: A month, how nice. Yes, son, go to Mexico, go far away from this rotten world. I'll follow you. I'll join you as soon as I can. And don't worry about writing. It's enough to know that you're now at peace.
LLUISET: Yes, Mamá, at peace.
DOÑA NURIA: For now, keep calm. As for me, as soon as I've taken care of some things about the house, you know, a few odds and ends of ours, I'll follow you. We'll be together there, and we'll be happy again . . .
LLUISET: Yes, yes, always . . .
DOÑA NURIA: Besides, I know you're going with your friend Ricard, who's a fine young man. You're going in good company. So don't you trouble yourself about me. I will keep very calm. And have a good crossing.
LLUISET: Thanks, thanks . . .

(*The* **COMMANDANT** *has reappeared.*)

COMMANDANT: Señora . . .
DOÑA NURIA (*Embracing her son*): Give me a kiss . . . another, one more. (*Pathetic kisses. Handing him the small bag.*) Here . . . Is it already time to set sail? Did the the ship's horn give the warning, captain?
COMMANDANT: Yes, señora, they're taking down the gangplank.
DOÑA NURIA; Then hurry . . . Goodbye, fill meu . . . Goodbye. Bon voyage! Bon voyage!

(*The* **COMMANDANT** *pulls* **LLUISET** *away gently.* **DOÑA NURIA** *takes a few steps and stops near the door.* **SHE** *is on the verge of collapse.* **SHE** *takes a small handkerchief from her pocket and waves it.*)

DOÑA NURIA: Adéu, ciao . . . Adéu, ciao . . . (**SHE** *is standing alone. Upstage the silhouette of the* **GUARD** *who watches her agape.* **SHE** *turns toward the barred window.* **SHE** *dries her tears and waves her handkerchief.*) Goodbye, adéu . . . (*Turning to the* **GUARD**.) How silly, I'm crying, when I know he's going to be happy in Mexico . . . but mothers are like that, you know? (*The* **GUARD** *is motionless as a statue.*) It's going to be a lovely spring day. The sea is beautiful. So gorgeous. It will be a smooth crossing . . . I'll be alone, all alone . . . with such a big house, so very big. All alone. But I'll go to Mexico, too . . . As soon as I get all the necessary papers. In the meantime (*Speaking directly to the* **GUARD**.) I'm going to be all alone. And my house is so large, just imagine, a house that's so old, so noble. But you know what I'm going to do? I'll take in lodgers.

It will be a guest house, as we call it in Barcelona . . . a house for guests. Gay young girls who sing, who laugh, who enjoy life. Yes, yes, I'll open a guest house in the middle of the Eixample . . . (*Crying again.*) That way I won't be so terribly alone, so terribly alone . . . until I can finally leave for Mexico, to rejoin my son . . . el meu fill! (*We hear the distant gunshots from below. And the sound of a ship's horn.* **DOÑA NURIA** *totters. The* **GUARD** *moves slightly. But then* **SHE** *stands up straight.* **SHE** *waves her handkerchief.*) They're sailling now, they're sailing . . . Adéu, ciao! . . . Adéu! Goodbye!

LIGHTS DOWN

Flor de Otoño, Teatro Español, Madrid, December 1982.
Set, costume and lighting design by Carlos Cytrinowsky.
Photo by Manuel Martínez Muñoz.

SOME NAMES, PLACES AND TITLES MENTIONED IN THE PLAY

"Baixant de la Font del Gat" — A song, or "copla," from a great popular success of 1924, *Baixant del Font del Gat o la Marieta de l'ull viu*, co-written and directed by the prolific Josep Amich i Bert (Amichatis) with Gastó A. Màntua.

Barrio Chino (Barri Xino) — The notorious red-light district of Barcelona, once known for its brothels, music halls, streetwalkers, transvestites, and drug trade. Jean Genet's *Thief's Journal* is one of several books that have helped to give the district its international fame.

Bataclan Cabaret — One of the most popular cabarets on the Paralelo in the 1920s.

The Born (Mercat del Born) — A vast wrought-iron market with skylights to provide natural light. Built in 1870, it was still a principal center of commerce in 1930.

Clavé Chorale (Coros d'en Clavé) — Josep Anselm Clavé was a nineteenth-century Catalan musician and patriot who promoted the performance of Catalan folk songs. The Orfeon Català was the most famous of the groups he inspired, but other choral groups among the working class used his name as a tribute.

La Criolla — Once the most famous cabaret in the Barrio Chino, at No. 10, Carrer del Cid, renowned for its drag and female performers. It was also known for its drug culture and gamblers and attracted diverse elements of Barcelona society.

The Eixample (The "ensanche" or "extension') — The planned expansion beyond the old city of Barcelona that began after 1850. A haven for the well-to-do, its streets offer some of the most impressive examples of Modernista architecture.

Maura (y Montaner), Antonio — Spanish politician and prime minister who began his career as a liberal and became a conservative. In 1909 he was removed from power because of the brutal suppression of an uprising protesting the drafting of Catalans to fight in Morocco. He returned to office in later years with coalition cabinets.

Montjuïc Prison — A castle-fortress-prison near the Barcelona harbor, on the crest of the hilly expanse known as Montjuïc. It became associated with Catalan oppression, and some of the surrounding areas were landscaped for the International Exposition in 1929.

Paralelo (Avinguda Paral.lel) — A major avenue that was the center of Barcelona night-life, with theatres, cabarets, and other enticing establishments. The name derives from the fact that it was laid out exactly on latitude 41° 44' north.

Poble Nou ("New Town") — A working-class district of Barcelona, adjacent to the Mercat del Born and north of the old city along the coast. At the time of the play it was known as a center of radicalism, but its character has changed drastically in recent years.

Sugrañes (Sugranyes) — The leading producer of variety shows in the French style at the Teatro Cómico on the Paralelo in the 1920s. Some of his hits were *Love Me*; *Oui, Oui*; *Ric, Ric;* and *Joy, Joy*.

Toti dal Monte — Internationally popular Italian coloratura soprano of the 1920s and 1930s. She is most remembered in the United States for her unorthodox casting as Madama Butterfly in a Victor recording of Puccini's opera with Beniamino Gigli.

TRANSLATOR'S NOTE

Autumn Flower poses more than the usual challenges to a translator recreating the play in English. It is distinctive in several ways, beginning with the character of its rash and ultimately noble gay protagonist. But it is also a play about a city, Barcelona, at a volatile time (1930) in its political and cultural history. Rodríguez Méndez evokes the period with frequent references to real people and places and daringly reflects the speech of the city in his shifts from Catalan to Castillian Spanish and the introduction of the differences in pronunciation of characters who have come to Barcelona from other regions of Spain. This, of course, affects the reception of the play in Spanish-speaking areas where Catalan is not spoken. His stage directions are unusually evocative of place, décor, and ambience, far beyond what many directors might deem essential. We also encounter unexpected words and deliberate turns of phrase that are ironic or parodic. For some, these stages directions will immediately recall those of Valle-Inclán's *Bohemian Lights*, which were once considered an impediment to staging—though obviously not to contemporary directors such as José Tamayo and Lluís Pasqual. In my English version I have retained a number of exclamations and other phrases in Catalan to suggest the language of the speaker and have indicated pronunciations at times that may or may not be implemented in production. "Señor," "Senyor," and "Senyó" are used to suggest the language and/or social status of the speaker.

Mindful of the numerous allusions and names that occur in the very successful plays of Tom Stoppard in the English-speaking theatre, I have cut only a few of the historic names in the play, knowing that the recognition factor will vary among spectators and readers. In two instances I have used Spanish place names rather than the Catalan nomenclature, since the playwright does the same and the Barrio Chino (Barri Xino) and the major avenue known as the Paralelo (Paral.lel) are widely known under those names. I have also provided at the end of the play a selective glossary of the names of people and places that occur in the dialogue and stage directions. For all the specific details of ambience provided in the descriptive passages that link the scenes of the play, *Autumn Flower* does not require such literalness for effective staging, and the use of actors in multiple roles will reduce what seems like a cast list for a period film to a reasonable and economically feasible number.

I would like to thank Richard Brad Medoff and Phyllis Zatlin for their careful reading of the second draft of *Autumn Flower* and noting some miscues from their own informed perspectives.

MPH

ABOUT THE TRANSLATOR

Marion Peter Holt is a writer, translator, and professor emeritus of Theatre and Spanish at the City University of New York. He has been a visiting professor of Theatre at the Yale School of Drama and at Hunter College (CUNY). His translations of Spanish and Spanish American plays have been staged in New York and London, in Australia, and by regional and university theatres throughout the United States. He has recently translated Sergi Belbel's *Blood* and Benet i Jornet's *Fleeting*. He is a member of the Dramatists Guild.

CRITICAL REACTION TO THE PLAY

"*Flor de Otoño* (*Autumn Flower*) is one of Rodríguez Méndez's most interesting plays from the perspective both of its content and its language. It takes place in the thirties, in the Ensanche (an elegant, upper middle-class neighborhood), and the Barrio Chino (the redlight district) of Barcelona, near the end of a dictatorship and just before the onset of the Republic."

>María-José Ragué-Arias
>*El teatro de fin de milenio en España*
>(Barcelona, 1996)

"In *Flor de Otoño*, a play that was made into a movie before it was staged, Rodríguez Méndez continues his fragmentation of space for the purpose of pursuing the action. The story of one of the most colorful transvestite performers of Barcelona's Barrio Chino gives rise to new reflections on this obscure area of recent Spanish history."

>César Oliva
>*El teatro desde 1936*
>(Madrid, 1989)

"Flor de Otoño is a sensational character. A great dramatic, or melodramatic, figure. The spoiled son of a wealthy Catalan family who, in a double life, slides from the Barcelona bourgeoisie to the lower depths of the Barrio Chino. Homosexuality, drugs, prostitution and anarchism, with all of their connotations of crime and terrorism."

>Lorenzo López Sancho
>*ABC* (Madrid), December 1982

"In my opinion, Antonio Díaz Zamora's production [of *Flor de Otoño*] has two important virtues that are often absent from the Spanish stage: stylistic unity and strong theatricality. . . . Carlos Cytrinowski's set design unhesitatingly introduces a series of elements that give the performance that vital, transgressive appeal to the senses, that visual depth that constitute theatricality."

>José Monleón
>*Primer Acto* (Madrid), December 1982

ESTRENO Plays is a series of stageworthy translations including works by J. L. Alonso de Santos, Luis Araújo, Fernando Arrabal, J. M. Benet i Jornet, Antonio Buero-Vallejo, Fermín Cabal, Ana Diosdado, Pilar Enciso, Antonio Gala, José López Rubio, M. Martínez Mediero, Lauro Olmo, Paloma Pedrero, Jaime Salom, Alfonso Sastre, Ramón del Valle-Inclán, Alfonso Vallejo, and other autors.

List price, nos. 1-11: $6; nos. 12-20 & rev. 6, $8; 40% discount to bookstores and dealers.

Visit our web page at www.rci.rutgers.edu/~estrplay/webpage.html or request our catalog by contacting:

Estreno Plays, Department of Spanish & Portuguese
Rutgers, The State University of New Jersey
105 George Street
New Brunswick, NJ 08901-1414
FAX: 732/932-9837   Phone: 732/932-9412x25
E-mail: estrplay@rci.rutgers.edu

Special offer: 3 or more volumes, $5 each. Mention this ad at time of order.